GOING
ALL
THE
WAY

The Real World of
Teens and Sex
****

GOING
ALL
THE
WAY

****
JERRY JOHNSTON

WORD BOOKS
PUBLISHER
WACO, TEXAS

A DIVISION OF
WORD, INCORPORATED

Unless specifically identified as factual, all names and events have been fictionalized for protection of privacy.

Library of Congress Cataloging-in-Publication Data

Johnston, Jerry, 1959–
  Going all the way.
  1. Sexual ethics for teenagers. 2. Sex—Religious
aspects—Christianity. 3. Teenagers—United States—
Sexual behavior. I. Title.
HQ32.J64 1988   306.7'088055   88-5474
ISBN 0-8499-0636-9
ISBN 0-8499-3100-2 (pbk.)

Printed in the United States of America
89801239 RRD 987654321

To my dear little

Danielle

eight years old and filled with so much
promise. And my six-year-old

Jeremy

a fine young lad who inspires his dad
to keep on going. And to

Jenilee

a two-year-old, with the mind and will
of a five-year-old,

    in hopes that you might avoid
    the pitfalls and scars of
    insincere relationships.
    May I ever show you agape love.

* * *

CONTENTS

* * *

INTRODUCTION

* * *

Get ready! What you are about to read reveals the stinging truth of what is going on with sex and teenagers. To paint the panorama, the overall network of moral demise has to be stated. It is nasty . . . but we cannot turn our heads any longer.

I simply could not remain silent. After almost every school assembly, a teenage guy or gal would come to me like a magnet, pouring out the lurid details. And now, three million students later, with hundreds of thousands of miles behind me, the anxiety and fear chiseled in their faces is like a haunting memory prompting me to speak out.

My detractors will blast me for writing this book. They will say what I have penned are "unmentionables." Like so many in the adult community they are convinced that by not "talking about it," somehow it will all go away. Yet, ignorance is not bliss and certainly not protection.

My only defense is that I have been where the kids are in over 2500 public schools. I have listened and audio-recorded their stories because they were so shocking. My orientation is secular youth and my heart bleeds for them and for the peace and purpose they are searching for through such diverse avenues.

Without exception, almost every teenager I talk with exclaims, "I can't talk to my mom or dad, Jerry." *Parental denial, gullibility, and indifference are the archenemies of many kids getting help or being deterred in time from poor sexual choice.* We just don't want to believe our little Suzi or Jimmy does those things. To avoid the stress of confrontation and reality, we choose to poke our heads in the sand. But facts are facts and the scenario is getting darker.

We must become informed. Because of the cunning removal of moral guideposts, young people have created their own set of standards in the love game. They no longer ostracize their friends if they are sexually active as they did in the '50s. At one time virginity was jealously guarded or vehemently lied about when lost. Tragically, now an uncommonly pure teenager lies to protect the very dirty little secret that she is still a virgin. According to *Psychology Today,* in the U.S. 11.5 million teenagers have had sexual intercourse. Of unmarried sexually active women, ages 15–19: 27 percent had never used any method of birth control; 34 percent had used a method consistently; and 39 percent had used a method but not every time. Four of every ten sexually active women became pregnant before they turned 20 years old. More than one in every 10 teenage women get pregnant each year.

Needless to say, venereal diseases are spreading like wildfire. *Nearly half of the estimated 20 million sexually transmitted disease patients are under age 25.* Ten- to 24-year-olds accounted for 62.5 percent of gonorrhea cases and 40 percent of syphilis cases in 1985.[1] The numbers keep rising. And, yet on the horizon, like a horror movie at its scariest scene, looms the AIDS epidemic. We can only wonder how things will be a decade from now.

We must educate kids. It is high time we talk to young people about sex. Parents need to sit down and talk to their teenagers. They must give sound guidance and, most of all, make crystal clear that they need to think first. A teenager must be fortified in the home to weather the storm of peer pressure and not to conform and let the standard down. Talk to your teenagers about anatomy, why God made the body as He has. Define to them what real love is and the purpose of sexual intercourse. It is not just for procreation, but enjoyment—in the proper setting. Answer questions on how far to go on a date, what to say to the if-you-love-me-let-me manipulation. Discuss sexually transmitted diseases in detail. Let them know the results of unwise decisions. It is up to you, the parent.

Accommodation is not the answer. Bettie B. Youngs, Ph.D., considered an expert in adolescent problems, states, "teenagers need to know how to assert their rights. They need to know not only that it is okay to say no to sexual intercourse but also why *it's okay to do so.*"[2] Regarding teenage homosexuality, she writes "both you and your child need to learn to cope with his homosexuality if it exists. Being gay is not something that the teenager is doing to hurt the parents. Nor is it in any way the parents' fault. Homosexuality is not an illness or a sexual perversion but rather a different sexual orientation."[3]

In *First Love, A Young Peoples Guide to Sexual Information,* Dr. Ruth Westheimer states, "Remember, whether you are straight or gay, you are a person of value to yourself and to other people."[4]

In *All Grown Up & No Place to Go* David Elkind states, "It is devastating for some parents at least, to discover that their son or daughter is gay. No rationalization or philosophy can ease the pain. Freud was very clear in stating that homosexuality was not an illness or sexual perversion but rather a different sexual orientation."[5]

Bluntly, let me say this philosophy is absolutely ridiculous and contributory to the massive problem facing us. It is false, totally false. Kids don't want the freedom of perverseness, but the security of restraint and proper guidelines. Is homosexuality sexual perversion? In every case of the gay teens I've counseled with, both lesbian and homosexual, they are riddled with guilt and want out. Read my chapter on homosexual practice (if you can get through it) and tell me if it is normal. Every line screams, "No, this is perversion!"

The majority of today's sex education is presently lacking the teaching of abstinence. Everyone seems to be afraid to tell kids that there are guidelines. I can assure you with this philosophy the time clock has already begun to tick toward the destruction of this future generation. But I see an even greater problem than this: the vast majority of teens I encounter who are having sexual problems, cannot truly define love. For this reason, I have closed the book with a definitive exegesis of one of the most familiar chapters in the Bible. When young people understand what true love is, they will understand the sham of all counterfeits.

It is my hope that this book will inform you of how the sexual revolution is impacting our teens, and what solutions are available to overcome its problems and consequences.

JERRY JOHNSTON
Kansas City

Part I

* * * * * * * * * * * * * * * * *

SODOM REVISITED

The Problems and Consequences
of the Sexual Revolution

To understand the real world of teens and sex, consider the impact that our sex-crazed society exerts on the average American teenager.

1

* * *

America Goes
All the Way

Popular rock singer George Michael on his music video, "I Want Your Sex," says, "In the past there were arguments for and against casual sex. Then it was a question of morality. These days it can be a question of life and death. It is as simple as that. And this song is not about casual sex."

Although misunderstood, this No. 1 hit song is not about sex with a lot of people, but sex with one person. In the music video Michael is writing, "EXPLORE MONOGAMY," on a girl's back as the lyrics pound out. Michael's philosophy relates that sex is natural, sex is fun, but it is best when it is one on one. The stark reality is that sex can also kill you. The song ends with Michael yelling out the command, "Have sex with me!" over and over.

The Problem

Sex is on the mind of America! For just a moment consider how our country and its populace is bombarded with every fascinating aspect of sex and the voluptuous female body. To understand the *real* world of teens and sex, we must perceive the incredible impact our sex-crazed society exerts on the average American teenager. The '50s are long gone with the naivité of knee-length, skirted girls blushing from embarrassment at the mention of the topic. Talk about how things have changed. What is happening now is like stepping into a different culture or world from that conservative era.

Attitudes, opinions, experimentation—and even curriculum—bespeak one message very clearly: a lot of people and particularly teenagers are doing it! For instance, at Centennial High School in rural Colorado, principal Mike Gomez was surprised with the news that exactly half the girls in the senior class were pregnant! Similar situations nationally have prompted school-based clinics in which contraceptives are given to students free of charge. Though the focus of political controversy, the number of school-based clinics is rising dramatically.

Brian, one sixteen-year-old frequenting his school clinic to receive condoms, candidly expresses his philosophy, "I don't want no little junior," he says, adding that his father had given him some good advice: "Don't leave it to the girl or luck."[1]

Sarah, who started having sex at 14, sought for birth control at her school clinic. To her mother, it was a relief. She stated, "I'd rather be shocked by the Pill than by a baby."[2]

What is the scenario really like? Hold on to your seat! It is not a sweet picture and the frightening aspects, as usual, are not reported as heavily as the promotion to go have fun.

* * *

America is going all the way. But all the way to where? While speaking at a major high school in a metropolitan city, I met Chrissy. The following is her story just as she told it to me.

Each account is coming directly from her lips. I was so stunned, I audio-recorded her story.

Chrissy represents the average teenage girl experimenting with sex. According to the National Center for Health Statistics, there were 270,922 unmarried girls who became pregnant in 1985 aged 15–19. There were 9,386 unmarried girls *under* 15 years of age who became pregnant in 1985.

Chrissy went through that and much more. Her story reflects too much, too soon.

* * *

Chrissy didn't look the part. The baby-soft features and comely innocence of her eyes belied a dark reality. Outwardly, she had all the attributes of a Joan of Arc in a high school play; but her appearance masked a secret life.

"I feel guilty as _____!" she blurted out, then she struggled to contain her emotions.

A single tear streaked down her cheek. I said nothing, simply waiting for her to continue.

"I just have to tell somebody what's going on in this lousy life of mine . . . I'm going to take a chance and trust you . . . ."

At first Chrissy looked like the kind of girl you'd find in the church choir. But the more she spoke, the more the torrent of negative feelings inside her washed away the facade to reveal a scarred ugliness. Not yet seventeen years old, Chrissy had already been sexually involved with more than 300 people.

* * *

I will tell Chrissy's story not to entertain you, but to draw a scandalous picture of what is going on in America today. In fact, I will tell you some of the shocking stories that thousands of other teenagers and young adults have shared with me about their lives. Since 1980 I have spoken face-to-face to more than three million high school students across North America. In cities of all sizes, in every state, to audiences both hostile and receptive, in small gatherings and in auditoriums crowded with thousands of teenagers, I have delivered my Life Exposé message. As I speak of the revolution going on in the lives of American youth—a revolution that has jarred our senses and erased our values—the kids react. They do not deny what I say or dispute my findings. Rather, they confirm the facts. And more. They tell me what they are doing, what they are thinking, and how they are coping.

Some people might conclude that I haven't met "typical" American teenagers, that the ones who confide in me are the extreme cases. I disagree. Though I have talked to kids from many different backgrounds, there is a common thread woven through their experiences. The strong currents which suck them into the whirlpool are the same. It is the national phenomenon that is driving teenagers, pre-teens, and even children to go all the way. Sex is no longer viewed as the preserve of adulthood, and this fact alone is changing too many lives, too fast.

✻　✻　✻

Thinking it might take some time to hear all of Chrissy's story, I rescheduled an appointment and audio-recorded our entire conversation. I had anticipated correctly. For more than two hours she poured out the incredible details of her sixteen years. When Chrissy was only ten, her father died. He was an alcoholic, and the booze finally took its toll on him. But that was only the beginning of the price his death would exact on Chrissy.

Her parents were divorced when she was only an infant, so Chrissy never lived with her father. She loved him despite the fact that he was a drunk—even though he never sent child support payments. And even though her mother cursed him at every opportunity. Still she loved him and enjoyed being with him. His sudden death plunged Chrissy into an abyss of depression. Having moved several times in just a few years, she already felt unsettled. Now things were worse than ever.

Chrissy didn't get along with her mother. They bickered constantly and found little common ground for reasonable discussion. Chrissy was convinced her mother distrusted and disliked her. Despondent and discouraged, she decided to seek the same pleasure she felt in being with her father. Chrissy chose the way of sex.

At a friend's house Chrissy had her first sexual experience. She was only ten years old, and though she was large for her age she hadn't yet entered puberty. Her teenage friends in the neighborhood were all a little older than she. One of them, a nineteen-year-old, was her first sexual partner.

"Having sex made me feel bad about myself," Chrissy confessed to me, "but I wanted so much to please somebody." At age eleven, life got even more complicated for Chrissy. Already involved sexually, she then turned on to drugs. First it was pot, then the harder stuff—cocaine, "angel dust," crack— "whatever I could get my hands on." So bad was her addiction, Chrissy turned on "before school, during school, and after school."

At some point when she was twelve years old, Chrissy started taking fewer drugs and doing more sexually. Every day for a period of a year and a half she had sex with at least one person. Often seeking out sexual partners, she would have intercourse or oral sex in cars, at home, or at school in darkened cloakrooms and auditoriums.

"I hoped so much for love, but I found it only once." Baffled by this, I asked for an explanation. "Well, I've only made love with one person, but I have had sex with many." Still confused, I insisted on more detail. Chrissy told me then that there was only one guy she ever really loved, and she considered him the only one with whom she made love, sexually. Strangely, she added that she had never, ever, had an orgasm. "That's something for marriage," she told me. "I won't let myself enjoy that until then, if I ever get married."

At age twelve, Chrissy became pregnant, by the same man with whom she had had her first sexual experience—she thinks. By then, he was one of many partners. Chrissy went to a free clinic and had an abortion performed. Her mother never found out. "I try not to think about it much, because I think it was murder. The baby would be four now, but I push that thought out of my mind whenever it comes. But it's real hard."

Chrissy's problems haven't gone unnoticed. Twice her mother placed her in girls' homes. She liked one, but was expelled for sleeping with one of the staff members, a twenty-eight-year-old man. At the other she stayed longer, but became increasingly depressed, and inside she ached deeply.

I asked Chrissy to tell me about the sexual exploits of her friends and classmates. Are they sexually active? Are you the exception or the rule? What's going on behind the scenes in your school and your neighborhood? Chrissy confirmed my suspicions, because it is the same story I've heard across America. "At least half the kids in our school are doing it," she said. "And not just the usual stuff. There are a lot of games, crazy parties, and some kinky things." By "kinky" she meant homosexual and bisexual involvement.

"Our group jokes around a lot about sex," Chrissy told me. "You know, like saying to some girl's boyfriend that you'd like to go to bed with him . . . just to tease. Of course, sometimes you really mean it and you want to seduce a guy."

And then she told me about the clubs. "Teen clubs, they call them. They don't sell any alcohol, but there's a lot of other things you can get there." These clubs are found in practically every major city I have visited.

To Chrissy, some things are out of the question, such as orgies and homosexual acts. But she has a surprising and contradictory tolerance in other areas. "Oh, I wouldn't hesitate to have sex with Boy George," she told me. "Even though he's admittedly bisexual?" I asked. "That wouldn't make any difference to me," she insisted, "because he's a really neat personality. And Prince is another I would go to bed with."

Going all the way for Chrissy is second nature now, but where's it taking her? I asked her pointedly, "Where's your life headed, Chrissy? How are you going to end up?" Almost without emotion she described for me one of her suicide attempts, when she punctured her wrists with a dull paring knife. "One of these times, that's probably what I'll do." "Take your own life?" I questioned. "Yeah . . . I think so."

* * *

How I wish you could have seen Chrissy. At sixteen years of age, she was as cute as a button and reminded me of a sheltered girl who sang in the church choir. Little did any of the teachers or adults around her realize the deep scars embedded in her mind.

Because of an absent father figure in her life, "sex with guys" became her attempted vehicle to fulfill the emptiness. Her goal in each sexual encounter was only to please her mate, in any way, like a slave.

Some people would call Chrissy a slut, but I am not one of them. To me she represents the victim of a dysfunctional family. When things "bombed" at home, she ventured out of the house groping for a sense of meaning and purpose. You may think Chrissy's story to be far-fetched, her experiences out of the realm of everyday life for most American teenagers. Guess again.

The Consequences

Going all the way has a price. You cannot be sexually active without exposing yourself to any of its several consequences:

Loss of virginity. Let's eavesdrop on an all-too-common conversation in a boy's high school locker room:

So, what did you get?
What do you think?
You're kidding? Really?
That was her first time? No way!
Yep, first time. I knocked her up and left her begging for
    more.
How about you, Dave? Ever bagged a babe?

Nope.
You're joking, right?
No.
Man, what are you, a faggot or something?

Virginity. What should be considered the highest virtue now makes one the object of ridicule. With many sexually inexperienced teenagers, virginity is to be hidden, lied about, never admitted. To be in college and never to have experienced sex is to be "naive," "innocent," "missing out," a "fundamentalist," or else gay. One fifteen-year-old admitted to becoming so tired of his friends' teasing that he went to a party, got drunk and asked an older girl to help him remove the stigma. This was an appealing little game to her, so she agreed. The guy, tense and unsure, could not perform. She attempted to engage in an oral sex act with him, but sent him away embarrassed and frustrated.

This problem is not unique to guys. One teenage girl confessed: "Later I got my nerve up and finally got laid. I was just so tired of getting _____ on I had to get it over with."

Losing virginity for many students is something they want "to get through with." Most of the time, the timing is wrong, the person is wrong and it means very little afterward.

Virgin brides are fast becoming an extinct species. According to *Redbook* magazine's 1987 Rate Your Sex Life survey, to which 26,000 women responded, some startling facts were revealed. Only about six percent of the women polled who are now under 25 were virgins when they married, compared to one-third polled a decade previously who were virgin brides.[3] *Redbook* states, "In the 1974 survey results, older women were also more likely than younger ones to have been virgins when they married, so what we are seeing is the continuation of a trend that has been steady for many decades. Not only are more of you experimenting with sex before marriage, but you are also starting to experiment at a younger age. Indeed, half of you first experienced sexual intercourse when you were 17 or younger—a jump from 39 percent in 1974. Another big change since the first survey is that now you are having sex with more partners. In 1974, for example, half of the women who were not virgin brides had had sex with only one man, their husband-to-be, and only 1 percent had had sex with more than six lovers. Today, only 23 percent of you who were not virgins when you wed had had premarital sex with only one man, and a full 32 percent of you have had six or more lovers. The significant change reflects the fact that more women are postponing marriage, and giving themselves more years in which to experiment with more lovers."[4]

There are certainly no hibernating hormones. To the contrary, it seems a significant number of people have their hormones in overdrive. With 78 million Americans single and prospective candidates for a relationship, much needs to be said.

* * *

Every week, thousands of teenagers rob themselves of the joy and sense of peace that come from waiting. Seventeen-year-old Susan gave away her virginity and was left without any recollection or meaning. "I got too drunk and got laid at a party. I didn't even know what I was doing. That's how it started. Once you've done it you just keep doing it."

The first time is special even if it's not a pleasant experience—because it is still the *first* time. But so many students carry acute guilt over the first time. I asked a high school girl in one of our assemblies what upset her most of all her sexual experiences: "Losing it, definitely. The first time it happens you feel really bad. You don't feel clean or pure anymore. After that, nothing is really very important to you."

Feelings like these are experienced by girls and guys alike. Frequently, the peer pressure is greater for guys and consequently "losing it" for a young man is met with congratulations and admiration. Even though this situation exists, it is not uncommon for guys to regret their first encounter and have to suppress their guilt over it.

Tim has had intercourse with many girls in his high

school career. He is preparing to graduate and yet these are his comments on virginity: "I think your virginity is very important. I was at a party one weekend and lost mine. I didn't care about the girl and I know she didn't care about me. I really wish I would have waited, but it's too late now."

It is common for young people to think that deciding to give up their virginity to their boyfriend or girlfriend will please their partner, show their commitment, and make the relationship more intimate. The opposite is true. Psychiatrist Martin Goldberg, M.D., director of the Marriage Council of Philadelphia observes that many of his clients find when a relationship begins with physical contact, it dies out faster than those built on good conversation and mutual interests.

There is an "innocence" that is lost when sex occurs the first time. Something special that was being reserved has now been handed out, leaving no unique gift to bring to a future fiancée. In a committed dating relationship or engagement, virginity is often exchanged. After all, thinks the individual, I am going to marry this person anyway. However, this situation creates an increased amount of stress due to fear that a breakup might occur, spoiling the "special" quality of that first time.

Sondra had been dating Jeff an entire school year. They were close. She was still a virgin, but as time went on, things began to feel so "right" for sex. One night after a date they went to his apartment and they made love for the very first time.

Soon after this, her body began to change. She was pregnant. They cried, then fought and finally broke up. She never wanted to see him again. He tried again and again to talk to her. It was over.

Their relationship had been very meaningful, but the pressure created by guilt and insecurity crushed their romance. Things may have been quite different had they waited to enclose their love life in the security and commitment of marriage. With no commitment to each other, the relationship crumbled under the weight of an unwanted pregnancy. Now Sondra has lost her virginity and her boyfriend. She is left to raise a child she loves dearly, but wishes had come much later.

Virginity is a condition that can be redeemed or traded for something in return. Most of the time, however, it is sold much too cheaply. Broken hearts and frustrated lives result.

Don is a senior who has slept with seven different girls in high school. "I can recall having to have sex with my first girlfriend. I was joked at, laughed at and called all sorts of names. After putting up with this, I finally gave in and had sex for the first time. After it happened and everyone found out I felt like an idiot—I had sex with this girl for all the wrong reasons. I did not wait for the right reasons."

Thousands of young people are anxiously awaiting the chance to get rid of their virginity. Others simply don't value it enough to say no if the opportunity occurs. Few really understand that "losing it" can be so devastating. Virginity may be lost, but the guilt, regret and apathy that result stay for a long time.

Sex is natural and should be fun, but for countless teenagers, sexual experiences are a huge disappointment. Young people seldom believe this until the stark reality sets in. Disillusioned by the feeling that sex wasn't what they anticipated it to be, many teens spiral into depression. To some, the despair over their inadequacy or poor "performance" leads even to suicidal thoughts.

Sex is oversold to an incredible extent. Rock music has been particularly successful in this erotic merchandising, tantalizing listeners and causing them to view sex as mystical, even spiritual. A high percentage of movies include explicit sex scenes which often have nothing to do with the plot. Others are filled with sexual innuendo. When movie stars make love to each other, viewers are provided with suggestions for their own fantasies.

Pornographic films are outrageously simplistic. Sex in a typical porno flick is not only expected but nearly always instantaneous. Partners always climax simultaneously. Orgasms are always explosive and multiple (for the woman). Ridiculous as these films are, they warp attitudes toward sex and create false ideas, especially when viewed by teenagers.

When teenagers first begin experimenting with sex, many must realize that things are not always as they seem. Kanda, a high school junior, said: "The first time was like no big deal at all. And now at parties it's almost always bang-bang and you never talk to them again. You both know you will never even admit doing it with each other." Kanda is now seventeen. She has slept with seven boyfriends and numerous "forgettables," as she calls them.

The pressure to experience the pleasure of sex is bad enough on American youth, but other factors compound the problem. Improper information, selfish partners, fear of discovery, lack of commitment, the absence of emotional intimacy and, very frequently, intoxication, combine to take a dreadful toll. The bottom line is an indescribable let-down. Yet how do the majority respond? They engage in more sexual activity, still seeking that special feeling they know is waiting for them with the "right" person: "You don't really know what the _____ is going on. The guy does all these things to you. I just thought, I guess this is what is supposed to happen."

One high school girl's first experience was marred by the fearful, hurried characteristic of premarital sex: "We were watching TV and then my parents went to bed. We went up to my room and started making out. He wanted to have sex so we got on the floor so there wouldn't be any noise. We were totally naked, doing it right in my room and my mom walked in and turned the lights on. It was terrible. Funny thing is, she just snapped, 'Get your clothes on' and then she left. She never said another word about it—still, it was a pretty _____ first time."

Like a tempting piece of candy, sex pulls at the feelings of America's teenagers. Many have told me they were willing to give up anything to try it, yet they found only great disappointment.

Suicide. Teenage years should be some of the most free, joyous years of life. For some, though, sexual experiences have created a tangled mess of emotions, leaving the kids bound in depression.

An attractive fifteen-year-old describes her experience: "It was so horrible, I just try to block it out of my mind. I loved him so much. I had known him since I was eleven, but he never even noticed me. Just recently he began paying attention to me. We hung around each other and one day I was in his living room. I was a little drunk. Anyway, he made love to me in his house while his parents were at work. I didn't really enjoy sex because I always thought it should be romantic and gentle. Instead it was tense. Even so, I felt happy afterward; it was a good start for me. The next thing I knew he totally ignores me. He didn't like me at all. I felt really used. I began smoking a lot. I didn't care at all about my appearance. I really wanted to die. How could this happen? Sex was supposed to be beautiful."

It is not uncommon for this disappointment to explode into a reckless "death wish." For innumerable kids, sex in the wrong way at the wrong time has been followed with a cloak of depression. For some it has even led to death.

Distrust and anger toward the opposite sex. Sex, as God intended, can bring two persons closer together in body and soul than any other human experience. Sadly, while sex is always a momentary physical union it can lead to a permanent emotional division, driving individuals apart through anger and distrust. Shari, age 16, described her experience: "My first time this guy who I thought liked me _____ me and then ignored me. That's it for me and sex. I don't trust guys. I don't trust my parents. I don't care."

Trust is the all-important factor, for sex is ideally suited to a committed, loving relationship that fosters trust. Marriage is the prime example of this relationship. The commitment and loyalty of marriage provides the perfect incubator for healthy, enjoyable sex. Yet this environment is totally lacking for sexually active teenagers. One seventeen-year-old described it this way: "I've slept with about seven guys. My boyfriend now is much different. We really love each other and have sex together. We've dated for two months and I've shared more with him than with anyone. If he ever broke up it would be really hard, I couldn't take it."

This girl's perspective—equating "two months" of dating with the intimacy of marriage—is quite common. But you can already detect a hint of distrust in her voice—"If *he* ever broke up"—a student's worst nightmare. Sex and dating do not mix well at all. To decide to have sex with someone brings the question of permanence. If the other breaks up, the entire sexual encounter becomes an unfortunate experience to be forgotten rather than cherished.

There must exist an environment of trust and commitment before sex can really be sex. When this condition is violated, then security is stripped away and anger takes its place.

Fear of inadequacy. Were you ever afraid of the dark? Do you recall the frantic childish imaginations that raced through your mind when you heard those infamous bumps in the night? Were you ever reluctant to hang your hand over the side of the bed, certain that some dreadful thing would pull you under?

Childhood fears fade as we grow to maturity. But for many adolescents, a more menacing form of fear comes to dominate their lives. For thousands of teenagers who've tasted the forbidden fruit of sexual pleasure, the aftertaste has been not only bitter but poisonous. They have been left with deep feelings of fearful insecurity, believing themselves to be inadequate. The anxieties can haunt with all the ferocity of a monster in the night. Yet few young people, if any, ever expect sexual involvement to end this way.

Young people are intimidated by the possibility of not matching up to someone else's performance. The teenager who is just beginning sexual experimentation will often fear comparison with other lovers whom his/her partner has slept with before. Since such a high percentage have multiple partners, this is inevitable. And it can be very cruel. The kids who have confided in me about their sex lives often describe a tense, artificial atmosphere in lovemaking with their boyfriends or girlfriends. To an impressionable teenager, our society seems to evaluate a person's worth on the basis of his or her sexual prowess. The spectre of not being able to perform like a sexual superstar can be terrifying.

Fear of pregnancy. The Number One Fear in the minds of many young people is pregnancy. Jeff, now twenty, revealed that he and his girlfriend have had sex many times, never using protection. The resulting fear has destroyed their relationship: "I know it was stupid not to use a condom, but we both felt wrong for having sex before marriage. Taking a condom on a date was like admitting I was 'planning' on it even when I was. That would just make us feel more guilty. *So* many times I thought she was pregnant. I mean once she missed a period and I was terrified. I had resolved in my mind that we were going to have a kid."

How vividly I remember fourteen-year-old Wendy, a freshman at a major metropolitan high school. She stayed to talk with me after one of my assembly programs. Several weeks before, her insistent, older boyfriend initiated Wendy into her first sexual experience. There was an uneasiness in her voice as she spoke. She said she feared being pregnant and waited intently for her period to come. Her days—and nights—were filled with fear.

Fear of disease. They call it "the clap." Its technical name, Neisseria Gonorrhea, is fittingly ugly. The simpler, more common term is gonorrhea. However stated, this disease is frightening. Yet it is just one of twenty-one rampant sexually transmitted diseases (STDs) ravaging our population today. "With stunning rapidity, new sexually transmissible diseases are surpassing previous scourges of venereal disease . . . One of four Americans between the ages of 15 and 55 will acquire a sexually transmitted disease at some point in his or her lifetime."[5]

Next to common colds and the flu, STDs as a group comprise the most prevalent communicable disease problem facing American society. Though penicillin has existed for forty years and VD clinics have networked and multiplied, nothing has succeeded in checking the soaring rates of VD cases in the past decade: "The estimated annual incidence of new gonorrhea and syphilis infections in the U.S. alone average out to a new infection every 10 seconds. Gonorrhea and syphilis alone account for more infections each year than measles, mumps, scarlet fever, strep throat, hepatitis and TB combined in the U.S."[6]

Because of a reluctance to discuss this topic, there is a general ignorance of the alarming rate of infection and the devastating results that occur from venereal diseases. More than anything, what has left researchers stupefied is the astronomical growth of new types of diseases previously unknown to the scientific community: "Sexually transmitted disease is epidemic. But it is not just the number of cases that is increasing— the past decade has seen a dramatic increase in new disease types: genital herpes, chlamydia and AIDS."[7]

This plethora of new illnesses has cut a swath of misery, pain and despair in the lives of millions of sexually active Americans. In the eyes of some victims, those who die from their disease have the easiest path: "I am a girl, eighteen. I had expected to get married this month. My boyfriend broke our engagement because I can't have children. A few years ago I ran with a crowd. We were all promiscuous. I contracted gonorrhea but didn't know it. Last month . . . the doctor found it. He said it will keep me from motherhood. I wish I were dead."[8]

What are these diseases and why are they so devastating? Let's examine the nature of STDs, their prevalence and the destruction they bring. As we do so, the sometimes gruesome price to be paid for careless sexual experimentation becomes evident.

The drip. Gonorrhea is so prevalent among the general public that health experts are warning that the welfare of the next generation is in jeopardy. Fifty percent of reported cases are among those under twenty-five years of age. In fact, between ten and twenty percent of American students will contract gonorrhea or another STD before they graduate from high school. More than one million new cases of gonorrhea are reported each year and experts estimate the true number is much higher.[9]

This disease is contracted through vaginal, anal or oral sexual contact and then proceeds through a two-to-ten-day incubation period before showing symptoms. Among men an involuntary drip of thick, yellow, puslike material may appear at the tip of the penis. Urination becomes painful. One study, however, found that sixty percent of men showed no symptoms of the infection. Women experience an inflammation of the fallopian tubes accompanied by severe lower abdominal pain and often an unpleasant vaginal discharge.

In most cases, gonorrhea is not only treatable, but curable. Antibiotics such as penicillin are used, although concern is growing over the fact that the disease is becoming more and more resistant to current doses of the antibiotic.[10]

In spite of the fact that gonorrhea may be treated, 80,000 to 100,000 women per year are sterilized by damage due to the infection. "Less frequently in advanced cases, the gonorrhea organisms will migrate through the bloodstream to . . . cause a crippling form of arthritis, meningitis of the brain, inflammation of the heart or damage to other body parts."[11]

Syphilis. With the introduction of penicillin, syphilis virtually disappeared. However, with the advent of birth control pills and radical changes in sexual activity, syphilis has reappeared. Each year 30,000 new cases are reported, although the true number is much larger.[12]

Once contracted, syphilis goes through a long period of being virtually unnoticed (no pain, occasional inconspicuous lesions or sores). Many people never discover the disease until many years after contracting it. "I am a 14-year-old girl. I have gone with boys since I was twelve and have fooled around a lot, but I am still a virgin and of that I'm very sure. I recently went to a clinic and the doctor told me I had syphilis. I am being treated for it now. . . . Other girls think they can't get syphilis without going all the way. I am telling you they can. I did some heavy petting and that's how I got it."[13]

Syphilis masquerades under the guise of many different diseases and consequently is difficult to discover. Sixty percent of its victims never suffer from the deadly "final stage" themselves, although they remain highly infectious for years. Those less fortunate victims are eventually attacked by the disease as it enters the "late" stage. Heart disease, ruptured arteries, diseases of the central nervous system, blindness, tumors and death all may occur in the victim who has unknowingly carried the "silent enemy" for years. Women having syphilis when they give birth may have infants who may quickly begin suffering from deforming blindness, insanity or death.[14]

Herpes. *Time* magazine called herpes today's "scarlet letter" and the "new leprosy." It is estimated that 20 million Americans have genital herpes with 500,000 new cases identified each year. Although the disease is not life-threatening, it is incurable. The victim periodically becomes infectious, a sign of which is the fresh outbreak of sores on the genitals, mouth or rectum. The disease contributes to guilt and fear over infecting partners, embarrassment, rejection and the hopeless feeling of harboring an incurable disease. The sores, when present, are painful and irritating, but the biggest impact of the infection is the alteration of lifestyle.

The *Time* article states: "As many doctors put it, 'It won't kill you, but you won't kill it either.' Herpes has changed the uneasy balance between sex for pleasure and sex for commitment. People are beginning to realize that romance is what it's all about. They're disillusioned with free sex and terrified of getting herpes and having it forever."[15]

An entire army. Besides the "big three" diseases—gonorrhea, syphilis, and herpes—an entire new army of STDs are invading our nation. Enter chlamydia: "Chlamydia is the fastest growing STD. Gonorrhea struck 2 million Americans last year; but chlamydia is estimated to have infected 3 to 4 million."[16]

This disease is much more stubborn than gonorrhea and

more difficult to treat. It causes sterility, tubal pregnancy and fetal death.

Another disease, papilloma, has been strongly linked to cervical cancer which killed 6,800 women in America last year alone: "Investigators in North America and Europe report that the papilloma virus is present in 90% of the cervical cancers sampled. . . . New evidence suggests that papilloma virus today is the fastest spreading sexually transmitted disease, with millions of new cases each year."[17]

On and on. It merely gets worse. Sixteen other STDs exist and are spreading across our nation, and particularly among our young people. The longer this plague continues, the more permissive teenagers become, the more these diseases will impact young lives.

Most teenagers in America will have their share of opportunities to engage in sexual activity. Those who give in to the temptation are taking a chance bigger than they could possibly imagine. With each new partner comes the ever-growing risk—a risk that becomes a reality for many millions each year. In fact, upwards of twenty percent of all teenagers in America will contract gonorrhea or another STD before receiving their diploma. The results are staggering: rejection, embarrassment, sores, lesions, sterility, tubal pregnancy, cardiovascular swelling, breakdown of the nervous system, blindness, insanity. And death.

AIDS. The reality is that sex has been "running scared" in recent years. When Air Canada flight attendant, Gaetan Dugas, traveled the world having countless affairs with homosexual men, little did he realize he would be the infamous catalyst to inject this disease into the bloodstream of North Americans. *San Francisco Chronicle* reporter, Randy Shilts, interviewed doctors in many cities and carefully discovered Dugas had been connected sexually with at least 40 of the first 248 AIDS victims in this country. Dugas often jetted in and out of Paris, where several cases of a mysterious fatal illness had been diagnosed as early as 1978. Health officials have concurred with Shilts's findings.

What is the result? When I spoke with Dr. Mead Morgan at the Centers for Disease Control in Atlanta, I was saddened to be informed that 237 teenagers, aged 13–19, now have AIDS. Furthermore, 11,653 people, aged 20–29, now are confirmed AIDS victims. But the truly shocking realization is that the incubation period of AIDS is three to five years. Only God really knows how many of the cited 10,840 victims contracted the deadly virus in their teenage years through sexual experimentation.

Dr. Morgan informed me that as of 14 March 1988, there are 135 people, aged 5–12 who have AIDS. But the area that makes you literally want to cry is the category 0–5, where the deadly AIDS virus claims and will soon kill all of its 762 victims. These are little children who scream out in the night with their bodies burning with fever. Their entire immune system breaks down each progressive minute, making them prey to a massive number of diseases. Ultimately, their minds will deteriorate before they develop to the point to articulate the horror they are experiencing.

These are, however, only conservative statistics. Dr. Morgan pointed out to me that 20 percent of the cases are never reported and another 15 percent are in the pipeline but not yet documented by the Centers for Disease Control. He also told me that there are 500 new cases of AIDS per week and the numbers associated with this deadly plague keep rising dramatically. To get the entire overview in our mind, we must realize that each month the escalation trend of this epidemic is exceeding the previous month. As of 14 March 1988, there were 56,212 Americans confirmed as AIDS victims excluding the 20 percent nonreporting sufferers. The breakdown by age categories is as follows: aged 30–39, there are 26,045 victims, aged 40–49, there are 11,665 victims, and over age 49, 5,715 victims.

The projection of new AIDS victims is scary to say the least. The Centers for Disease Control is projecting 33,000 new cases in 1988; 45,000 cases in 1989; 54,000 cases in 1990; and 74,000 victims in 1991.

Conservative projections mean that there will be over 270,000 people with the AIDS virus in the United States by 1991, charting from the year 1981.

Added to these very sad statistics are the 31,420 people who have already died of AIDS as of 14 March 1988. Of this number, 525 individuals were 13 years of age or younger!

Michael Stone died three months after he finally was diagnosed with AIDS. At 19, he was the first AIDS patient believed to have contracted the disease while in high school in San Francisco. Michael was a National Merit Scholar at the city's top academic high school, Lowell High School. He was a confident and aggressive youth. Michael early dismissed the symptoms of his disease: the prolonged swollen lymph glands, diarrhea and oral fungus. Like so many teenagers, he rejected the possibility that he could get AIDS even though he was gay and both his parents and doctor had warned him he was at risk.

"In San Francisco alone, an estimated 4,000 San Francisco high school students may already be carrying the virus without knowing it. 'What we're seeing now is like a delayed photograph of what was actually present three to five years ago,' says Paul Gibson, a San Francisco Health Department educator who has frequently given classroom lectures on AIDS."[18]

* * *

Every time a teenager says yes to sex, the trigger is pulled in a harrowing game of Russian roulette. Unfortunately, more than one chamber is loaded.

So many teenagers are cornered, paralyzed by fears— the fear of inadequacy, the fear of pregnancy, the fear of disease—all of which are consequences of the sexual revolution. Yet they still continue. Relentlessly they remain active until overcome by fear or until the worst anticipation becomes a reality. A soft-spoken, raven-haired sixteen-year-old added this sad commentary about going all the way: "After I lost it, I didn't feel pure anymore. After that wore off, all I've ever felt since is fear."

2

* * *

Kids Having Kids

"There are two kinds of sex that I'm talking about," says Rae Dawn Chong in a new video, "intercourse and anal intercourse . . . that's why guys gotta wear condoms . . . and girls gotta make sure guys wear them . . . each time you have sex with someone new and you don't use a condom, you're taking a risk with your life . . . don't take that risk."[1]

Rae Dawn's blatantly raw words are from the script of *Sex, Drugs & AIDS,* an eighteen-minute film being shown in thousands of American public schools to teens as young as fourteen years of age. Even for the most streetwise kids, some of the scenes are shockingly explicit. "But," Chong matter-of-factly observes, "this isn't 1957." The producers of this public service program contend that its directness is necessary, since the sexual revolution has carried us so far, so fast.

* * *

The posters hanging in high schools where I speak are attempting to get the kids' attention. One poster shows a side profile of a teenage girl carrying her books who looks gigantically nine months pregnant. It says, "Will Your Child Learn to Multiply Before She Learns to Subtract?" Another has a seductive Tom Selleck-looking high school guy cooing, "Trust Me. I Won't Get You Pregnant." The cut-line reads, "Before you fall for a line like this, call us for help." Perhaps, the most touching is the poster that has what looks like a very innocent sophomore or junior girl disappointedly saying, "He said if I didn't do it, he wouldn't love me anymore."

The Problem

Teenagers are sexually active, more active than many adults can begin to imagine; and the evidence speaks for itself. United States teenagers are more sexually active than any other nation on the face of the globe. The Alan Guttmacher Institute revealed that the number of pregnancies per 1,000 girls, aged 15–19 (with similar rates of sexual activity) are: 96 per thousand in the United States as compared with: Canada, 44 per thousand; England, 45 per thousand; France, 43 per thousand; The Netherlands, 14 per thousand; and Sweden, 35 per thousand. Every day in America—every day—more than 3,000 teenaged girls become pregnant! More than one million every year! Of this number, more than 80 percent are unmarried. And more than half of the babies are aborted.[2]

One large Chicago high school, DuSable High, recently reported that one-third of its female students were pregnant. That same school has decided to deal with the crisis by providing counseling services and contraceptives.[3] The revelation of this practice brought media exposure about similar programs in scores of other cities.

The spectre of AIDS has brought a whole new element into this problem of promiscuity. Now sexual activity can even result in death. Not only are the children conceived being killed, so are some of their young parents—in alarmingly higher numbers.

According to an extensive poll conducted by *People* magazine in 1987, the average American teenager is initiated to the sexual experience at age sixteen. Fifty-seven percent of teens polled said they had lost their virginity in high school. (This poll coincides with the majority of other statistical evidence by numerous adolescent experts and sexologists across the U.S., namely, that one in every two teens has "gone all the way" before he or she walked across the platform in the graduation ceremony to receive a high school diploma.) Often prompted by peer pressure or curiosity, most teenagers don't stop after the first attempt. Most teens who do indulge claim to be quite active and many boast of skilled technique. Twenty-two percent of the teens and forty-four percent of the college students say they have sex at least once every three weeks.[4] However, only thirty-nine percent of high school teens admit to using any contraceptives while having sex.

For concerned teenagers, the most frightening aspect of having sex is the risk of unwanted responsibility—especially the responsibility of making monumental, life-altering decisions. Teenagers wonder . . .

If I get pregnant, will I get an abortion?

Does getting pregnant mean it's best to get married?

Could I bring myself to tell my parents?

These and a thousand other questions bombard the mind. Yet, a startlingly significant number of other teenagers do not think about these matters at all. They continue to have sex without contraceptives. Some act out of ignorance. Others are intimidated by a guy's refusal to use what they consider to be pleasure-restricting condoms. Many are, remarkably, of the persuasion that "it won't happen to me."

People's study revealed that less than fifteen percent of the teenagers would bear and raise a baby out of wedlock. The vast majority see abortion as the obvious—and only—solution to their unfortunate situation. They don't like the idea, but it seems the only alternative which doesn't mess up one's lifestyle. One California teenager said, "I was _____ off when I found out I was pregnant. Getting an abortion . . . was the best thing I could have done."[5] A girl in Ohio expressed her feelings: "I couldn't believe I was lying on that table and was actually asking them to kill my baby. To kill it and take it from me like it was something filthy and rotten. But I did it. I did it and it's over. Sometimes I have to keep telling myself that it's over."[6]

But what is it that's really over? Sex, Risk, Pregnancy, Abortion. Sex, Risk, Pregnancy, Abortion. Is this the inevitable cycle? Will it go on and on with more lives being affected every day? Can anything be done to stop it? Many say that education is the key, especially straightforward education like Chong's film. And what about parents? What can they do? And, what do they really know? Cheri, a seventeen-year-old Atlanta senior said, "Our parents just know we're out there _____ our little buns off, but they can't bring themselves to talk to us about it."[7]

The Consequences

In conversations and interviews with literally thousands of teenagers and parents across North America, I've heard firsthand the trauma brought on by premarital sex.

✳   ✳   ✳

Tonight, as she has for several haunting nights, fourteen-year-old Denise lies awake rehearsing how she will tell her father. Repeatedly, her mind freezes like a video frame on stop-action. She imagines that some unknown force is manipulating her by remote control. Denise doesn't know what to do next. Her jaw tightens as she thinks of Ronnie. He's gone. All his promises to pay for the abortion were just words that came as easy to him as his insistence that she "prove her love" by having sex.

Denise is an eighth grader with $70 trying desperately to hide the inevitable from her father. That night in Ronnie's bedroom has played through her mind so many times. It has no color, no life, everything is just a pale gray memory. *Why me?*, she wonders. Denise never thought this could happen to her. Never.[8]

A sad story. Yet so commonplace. In fact, it will be re-peated in various forms several hundred thousand times a year in America.

A high percentage of these teens have never received any sex education from their parents. Many so poorly understand the instruction they have received in school, they think, "It couldn't happen to me."

This is evidenced by the fact that at least three-fourths of all teenage pregnancies are unintentional. For many girls preg-nancy is the unwelcome result of their earliest, and often their first, sexual experiences. "It's not a pretty picture. It's not a TV soap opera either. The reality of pregnancy outside of marriage is scary and lonely. To have premarital sex was my choice one hot June night, forcing many decisions I thought I would never have to make. Those decisions radically changed my life."[9]

Pregnancy is a demanding responsibility when the girl is married. Being fourteen, in school, unmarried and frightened, as Denise was, makes it an almost unimaginable strain. For many of these kids, there isn't an adequate support system.

In the last twenty years, the rate of illegitimate births has skyrocketed from 15 to 51 percent. Even worse, 60 percent of the teenage girls who are pregnant today in America will be pregnant again in the next two years.[10]

About half of the girls decide to give birth. The others—approximately 400,000 teens—choose the darker but easier path. Believing it's not worth the trouble, they opt to abort the pregnancy. Another 100,000 girls have miscarriages, ending their pregnancies. Of the 490,000 who have their babies, 96 percent decide to keep them. For many of the 470,000 unwed mothers, this locks them into a life of struggle and hopeless-ness.[11]

For the girl who cannot bear the thought of parting with her child, there is usually a grueling path ahead. Keeping the baby and attempting to provide a home is no simple matter. Of the girls who keep their babies, 80 percent become high school dropouts. More than 60 percent are forced to go on welfare since the average income of America's unwed mothers is approximately $4000.[12] These figures are especially alarming within black society, where 41 percent of teenage girls are pregnant before they turn twenty. Of these teens, 87 percent are not married.[13] Dr. William Pierce, of the National Committee for Adoption, characterizes the young single mother's future as "a life of hopelessness and despair."[14]

"Because the entire ordeal occurs outside the warmth of any kind of loving, committed relationship such as marriage, the young girl ends up shouldering the heartache and guilt without any support at all: Parents occasionally will drop a daughter off at Gladney Home and not want her back; rejection by boyfriends is almost universal. He was able to go on and play softball, work, stay with his family and friends."[15] "My boyfriend kept pursuing me for sex . . . I had sex with him thinking that I owed it to him . . . Later when I learned I was pregnant he blew up, said to get an abortion, and that it was all my fault."[16]

Relatively few unwed mothers choose to give up their children for adoption, but those who do endure a heart-tearing trauma. One little mother, on the verge of releasing her newborn for adoption stated: "He kept crying and crying, and finally, when I rocked him, he stopped and opened those eyes real big and he looked at me. I went, 'Ohhhhh.' He had eyes like my brother. Gray eyes, long lashes. That's when I started crying. I said, 'Get the nurse and tell her to come get him. I can't stand this anymore.'"[17]

The fortunate ones get married. Or so it seems at first. The 220,000 girls who follow their pregnancy by a hurried marriage usually sink deeper, with the divorce rate for these couples being twice as high as the average.[18] The disruptive forces confronting these precarious young marriages are often overwhelming. Lack of money is only one of a multitude of problems.

Karen Walters, sixteen, and James Ritenour, nineteen, are spending this Saturday night watching Hulk Hogan on TV in

St. Agnes Hospital with their two-day-old infant, Tanya Rene. "When I get out we'll celebrate," says the new mother. "We're too young to go to a bar, so I guess we'll hang out in the mall."[19]

*   *   *

Unplanned pregnancies cause teenagers to make potentially life-changing decisions. Do I keep the baby? Do I shelve my long-term education plans? Do I risk rejection? Do I give my child away? These are decisions that force "kids" to be adults before they are emotionally and mentally ready.

3

***

The Killing Fields

22,000,000 Murders*
without a Conviction

The Problem

Jennifer peered cautiously around the drugstore to make sure there was no one she knew among the customers. Her eyes continued to dart nervously back and forth as she waited in the checkout line. In her hand were three objects: two large boxes of facial tissues and a smaller box containing an early pregnancy test. Jennifer used the tissues to conceal the other product, like a cardboard sandwich. Still jittery as she paid for the purchase, Jennifer couldn't wait to get out the door. She did not want someone she knew to see what she was buying,

---

*And still counting. According to National Right to Life from Roe vs. Wade in 1973 through 1987 there have been more than 21,296,898 legal abortions performed in the U.S.

even though she had traveled miles across town. Finally, her three boxes safely hidden in a brown sack, Jennifer hurried back to the car where Cindy, her best friend and volunteer chauffeur, waited patiently. When Jennifer's door slammed shut, they both sighed loudly.

At Cindy's house Jennifer carefully followed the directions on the pregnancy test. The result was exactly what she did not want it to be: positive. She was pregnant. As the two girls, both juniors in high school, stared at the indicator strip, the air grew heavy.

"Why me?" Jennifer burst out, her eyes fixed on the ceiling.

She repeated her plaintive cry, "Why me?" The question now was tinged with more pathos, more intensity.

Cindy was uncharacteristically quiet, obviously feeling the weight of the dilemma. "Are you going to tell Brad?" she asked.

Jennifer didn't hesitate a second to reply, "Of course, I am. After all, it's *his* fault!"

Upon hearing the news, Brad expressed little compassion for Jennifer. Rather, he was brusque with her, even suggesting doubt that he was really the father. Marriage was, of course, out of the question. "I've got my whole life ahead of me," he explained, "and this just isn't in the plan." From his point of view, the solution was obvious: get an abortion. "It's not yet a baby anyway," Brad pronounced.

In her heart, Jennifer knew it *was* a baby. She struggled desperately with that fact, thinking of all the implications for herself, her family, and her future. She feared embarrassment, the loss of respect, and the scuttling of her academic goals. Her thoughts were dark, bleak. She could see no possibility of being a good mother at her age. She seethed with deep hatred toward Brad and deeper anger with herself for having given in to him. She loved her parents, but just couldn't bring herself to hurt them. They must never, ever find out, she resolved.

Cindy offered to go with Jennifer to the abortion clinic. "You can ask them if you really ought to have one," Cindy tried to reassure her. "I'm sure they have to tell you." But

Cindy and Jennifer had both heard too many stories about other girls to actually believe that.

Within a month the girls had developed a plan. They forged excuse slips and skipped out of their afternoon classes. Jennifer had made arrangements to spend the weekend at Cindy's, so she wouldn't be at home after getting the abortion. The ten miles they drove seemed to be an interminable distance. Their destination was a clinic recommended by Planned Parenthood. Jennifer had phoned their office to request information for "a friend."

Expecting a sensitive, caring place, Jennifer was severely disappointed. The people were very businesslike, stoically detached. In spite of all the questions spilling out of her mind and heart, Jennifer met no one whom she really wanted to ask anything. She filled out a few papers, paid her $310 fee (which she had taken out of her savings account), went to a designated room, and waited her turn.

Every moment she spent in the gray solace of the clinic room, Jennifer thought not about *what* she was doing but *who* she was expelling from her body, her life. By the time the doctor and nurse arrived, Jennifer was in tears, trembling with anxiety. The nurse said, "It's OK . . . you'll hardly feel it. We're just going to remove a little tissue."

The Attempted Justification of Abortion

Abortionists, or as they prefer to be called, "pro-choice advocates," are quick to argue that women must have the right to remove that "little tissue" from their bodies. To prevent "unwanted" children or to prevent the grief from "defective" children, they see abortion as the only reasonable alternative. They assure us that it is better for all concerned, particularly for teenagers who need to be doing other things besides raising kids. The philosophy is quite simple: Get rid of the "little tissue" and get on with your life. More than half of pregnant girls make this choice.

By the time Jennifer missed her first period, the "little tissue" inside her already had a beating heart, feebly but discernibly pumping with the first signs of life. By the time Jennifer went to the abortion clinic, the "little tissue" weighed about one-thirtieth of an ounce. The hands and feet were well formed and distinctly human . . . The taste buds in the mouth had begun to form. The upper and lower jaws were synchronized in development. The adrenal and thyroid glands were functioning.[1] No one at the abortion clinic bothered to tell Jennifer any of these things, nor did they even ask her if she was certain about having the abortion.

How can the pro-choice forces justify the destruction of such a fetus? They contend that a fetus is not really a person in the truest sense. The primary concern, they argue, is a woman's right to privacy. It is not a personal or moral issue, but a political and social issue.

The Supreme Court in 1973, unfortunately, legitimized this view, by making abortion on demand the law of the land. All the major legal judgments since then have served only to compound that tragic verdict. Gone are the rights of parents. Gone are the rights of the baby. Today in the United States, it is perfectly legal for a minor child to have an abortion without her parents' knowledge or consent. But, technically, she cannot have her ears pierced without their permission!

Abortionists say that children who result from incest or rape, children who are born with physical defects, cannot live full and worthwhile lives. And many dare to imply that the majority of abortions in America prevent these tragedies from occurring. This is a monumental lie. Less than five percent of abortions in the U.S. involve the victims of incest or rape, or mothers whose lives are endangered by pregnancy. U.S. Surgeon General, C. Everett Koop, says, "Protection of the life of the mother as an excuse for an abortion is a smoke screen. In my 36 years in pediatric surgery I have never known of one instance where the child had to be aborted to save the mother's life."[2] The vast majority of abortions are performed simply because a child doesn't figure into the plans.

*   *   *

"The suction tube, about the size of a thick ball point pen, was taken from its sterile container and inserted through the dilated cervix up into the uterus, where it finally punctured the sac surrounding the child, allowing the amniotic fluid to escape.

"Then the instrument found the child. Neither Jennifer (sic), the abortionist, the anesthesiologist, nor the attending nurse were aware of the drama that was taking place just a few inches from each of them.

"Slightly under twelve weeks of age, the tiny baby was already fully developed in its major features. Its little heart was pounding at 140 beats per minute until the shiny steel arm burst into the baby's warm home. The heart rate raced to over 200 beats per minute as the child jerked and recoiled from the viciousness of the blade. It was a futile effort. The tiny, wonderful form was torn from its home, piece by piece.

"The head was too large to be pulled in one piece by the suction tube. The abortionist employed a polyp forceps . . . grasped it tightly, crushed the head, and then removed the fractured pieces from the womb.

"The womb was sucked clean of the remaining shattered pieces and the ordeal was over."

The doctor spoke briefly with Jennifer (she had never met him before) and gave her a packet of birth control pills and medicine to prevent infection. Shortly thereafter, Cindy helped her out to the waiting car and sped away.

What Is Abortion?

Last year in this country, Jennifer's experience was repeated more than one million times. Since 1973, when the U.S. Supreme Court ruled in favor of abortion on demand, there have been more than 22 million abortions performed in this nation. The techniques have differed, but the result is the same: a life is snuffed out, and usually for the sake of convenience.

Different terms have been developed to describe various kinds of abortion. A "therapeutic" abortion is performed when the mother's physical health is at stake; a "psychiatric" abortion, for her mental health. "Eugenic" abortion keeps retarded or deformed children from being born. "Social" abortion is for the purpose of easing economic pressures on a family. "Ethical" abortion is utilized in cases of rape or incest. But, far and away the most common form of abortion in the United States is "abortion on demand," for which there need not be any discernible reason. Some feminists have referred to this as "voluntary miscarriage."

One authority on this subject, Gary Bergel, describes the five principal means of abortion in America:

D & C. This method—the letters stand for Dilatation and Curettage—is most often used in the first thirteen weeks of pregnancy. D & C is performed with a small, hoe-shaped instrument which is inserted through the dilated cervix. The abortionist uses this tool to scrape the baby's body off the uterine wall.

Suction. For early-term pregnancies, this is now the method of choice. Developed in Communist China, the suction technique is very simple: a tube is placed into the womb and the baby and placenta are sucked into a jar. Practitioners say this is a much neater, more preferable method.

Salt Poisoning. Through a long needle thrust in the mother's abdomen, a strong salt solution is injected into the amniotic fluid surrounding the child. The salt poisons and burns the baby to death. A short time later, the mother goes into labor and delivers a grotesque, dead baby. However, some of these "salt babies" have survived and have been born alive.

Caesarean Section. In the third trimester abortions, this method is used. Surgically entering the womb through the abdominal wall, the abortionist removes the baby from its place. Usually, the fetus is then left to die on its own from neglect. Sometimes, the fetus has to be deliberately killed.

Prostaglandin Chemical Abortion. This newest form of abortion uses hormone like chemical substances which cause the muscles of the uterus to contract and push the baby out prematurely. Unfortunately, frightening side effects have been recorded. Some babies have been decapitated. A few mothers have accidentally died from cardiac arrest induced by a chemical reaction. Despite these complications, the Upjohn Company, developer of this drug, contended in their recent annual report that they would continue to refine these abortion compounds in India and China.[3]

The Consequences

On average, every day more than 3,600 young girls like Jennifer endure an experience like hers. Each one represents at least one life ended.

The booming one half *billion* dollar abortion industry is raking in enormous profits.[4] In the typical clinic, everything is handled so smoothly that one might forget what is really happening. Of course, this is part of the strategy. No one stays afterward to see the dreadful result of this dirty business. The back rooms of abortion clinics can turn into veritable graveyards after too many fetuses pile up.

"I am a housewife and a registered nurse from Jacksonville. I retired from the nursing profession when I became pregnant with my first child and stayed retired until my fourth child was in the sixth grade. I then returned to work in my local hospital. Many things progressed in those years— some things regressed. I worked the 11:00 PM to 7:00 AM shift, and when we weren't busy I'd go help with the newborns. One night when I went to the nursery I saw a bassinet outside the nursery. There was a baby in this bassinet—a crying, perfectly formed baby. But there was a difference in this child. She had been scalded. She was the victim of a saline abortion. This little girl looked as if she had been put in a pot of boiling water. No doctor, no nurse, no parent to comfort this hurt, burned child. She was left alone to die in pain. They wouldn't let her inside the nursery—they wouldn't even cover her. It's hard to believe this can happen in a modern hospital—but it does. All the time. I asked a nurse in another hospital what they do with their babies that are aborted by saline. They put the infant in a bucket and put the lid on. Suffocation! Ladies . . . gentlemen . . . please . . . ."[5]

The wreckage is shocking, the calculated cruelty horrifying. Day after day hundreds of garbage bags, filled with scalded little bodies or bloody strips and fragments, are sealed, packed and dumped like rotten vegetables. We wince at the killing fields of Cambodia and the mindlessness of genocide. Yet this crime is far greater, snuffing out more lives.

No one, certainly not I, dare say teenage pregnancy is not a crisis in America. Nor can it be denied that an expectant, unmarried sixteen-year-old is an embarrassment to her family. It is obvious that she may seriously jeopardize her college and career. But what of the one who is so often forgotten—the little life growing inside the womb? Current "reasoning" says that personal rights don't exist for one living there.

* * *

Jennifer didn't have to go through with the abortion. But she gave in to the strong personal and societal pressures facing nearly every girl in America. She believed the lie. Temporarily, she convinced herself that everyone would be better off. No one told her that she would possibly go through severe depression as a result of her actions. There was no counsel given, positively or negatively, about anything. She may as well have been a dumb animal being treated by the local veterinarian. After two uncomfortable days at Cindy's place, she went back home. On Monday morning she returned to school. She forced herself to act as if everything were back to normal, that she had simply closed an unfortunate chapter in her life. She soon learned it wasn't really that simple.

* * *

There are other consequences. So many teenage girls are told lies, coddled and goaded into having an abortion. It makes so much sense, they are told. But inside, deep in the heart, nearly every one of these young mothers knows that abortion is the taking of a life. It is murder in the first degree. Here's what one wrote:

Dear Sir:

My abortion is something I wish I had never done. I can remember looking at the doctor when it was done and I saw him putting my baby in a plastic bag and then throwing it away in a garbage bag. Have you ever lost something you dearly loved? I did, and I'm not proud of it. I can tell you, having an abortion is killing me slowly.[6]

Another wrote: "There was discomfort and a little cramping, but there was something far deeper. It was an elusive emptiness that had invaded her whole being . . . it was a crushing feeling of total defeat in the only significant battle she'd ever fought."[7]

* * *

These are the facts: Living human beings with all the vital organs and functions have been labeled "potential life." Arbitrarily they are singled out and destroyed. What's worse, it is done for profit. Apparently, as long as judges remain blind and as long as the medical profession garners hundreds of millions of dollars annually, abortion will remain America's fatal solution to one problem of the sexual revolution.

4

* * *

Who's That Playboy
in the Penthouse?

In 1955 Hugh Hefner was an obscure but zealous man determined to build a new kind of publishing empire. Though he had little money and less influence, he had one unusual asset: a color photograph of Marilyn Monroe—in the nude. With that as his first enticing centerfold, Hefner produced the pilot issue of *Playboy.* From the outset it was admittedly clear: *Playboy* is not just a magazine, it is a philosophy, a statement about life. Hefner himself was bent on becoming a virtual synonym for hedonism.

Today, more than a quarter of a billion dollars strong, Hugh Hefner does rule an empire. His kingdom encompasses a lustful world of casinos, resorts, television networks and ever-popular publications. More significantly, he has succeeded in communicating the gospel of sexual "freedom" to America. From the gaudy confines of his Beverly Hills mansion, clad in tailored pajamas and surrounded by nearly naked admirers, Hefner lives out what he once fantasized. Openly, even defiantly, he relishes his role as the man responsible for ushering in a new era of liberated thinking. And he has done it with more than pictures. Editorially, *Playboy* has systematically and articulately undermined once-sacred standards of morality and ethics.

The Problem

With Hefner's bold success as a motivator, other sex merchants have flooded the market with their fleshly wares. To meet the ever-increasing, never-satisfied appetite of buyers, the magazines continually try to outdo their competitors and themselves. Compared with today's pornographic products, the first issue of *Playboy* seems relatively decent.

How big a business has this become? It is now at least a $5-billion-a-year industry, earning more than the legitimate movie and record companies combined. At least half a dozen of the most popular monthly magazines in America are for-men-only publications. *Playboy* and *Penthouse*, for example, boast circulations far exceeding *Time* and *Newsweek.*[1] "Adult" periodicals are a major influence on the lives—and budgets—of millions. Unfortunately, a frighteningly high percentage of readers are not adults at all, but teenagers and children who have grown up prematurely on a diet of carnal knowledge. Many are able to pick through the pile of filth at local convenience stores; others manage to sneak a peek at their father's collection.

Hustler, the porn magazine with the third highest readership, is indescribably perverse. Known best for its action close-ups of the sex organs, *Hustler's* rawness is blatant and purposeful. Other features glorify the despicable, like the cartoon strip, "Chester the Molester," which belittles child abuse.

Hustler publisher Larry Flynt defends his magazine's content as an expression protected under the U.S. Constitution. In a debate with noted law professor William A. Stanmeyer, carried by a Chicago television station, Flynt said to

Stanmeyer, "You wouldn't want to censor a discussion of sex like this program. Then why do you want to censor *Hustler?*" Stanmeyer replied, "If *Hustler* magazine is merely 'a discussion of sex,' like a gynecology text, then let the cameraman focus back there where the producer has a copy; zoom in on the pictures that *Hustler* contains, and give the people of Chicago a close-up. Let them decide whether *Hustler* is just a medical text."

Stanmeyer describes what happened next: "The reaction to this brazen challenge was consternation in the glass-walled control booth: hands signaling, 'No, No, Don't!': grimaces conjuring up angry F.C.C. lawyers; faces anticipating angry phone calls from the audience."

Child Pornography

How twisted are the pornographers? The Commission on Obscenity and Pornography appointed by President Reagan discovered more than 300 magazines devoted to "kiddie porn." What is "kiddie porn"? This trash features children, from toddlers to young teens, in explicitly erotic photographs and films. *Lollitots* and *Moppets,* two of the best-selling magazines in "adult bookstores," display naked, spread-eagled children ages three to fourteen. Many of the photos depict sexual acts. Very brief, but very expensive ($20 average for just 200 feet of film), "kiddie porn" films have titles such as: "Daddy's Little Girls" and "Desires with Young Girls."[2]

The majority of these children are the unwanted offspring of addicts and drifters. Left to fend for themselves, yet without any skills, they are drawn into the sleazy world of porn with promises of food, affection, even fame—all in return for "acting" in a "movie."

Father Bruce Ritter is a Franciscan priest who rescues runaways and castaways from the streets of New York City. He is a magnificent man who is doing a marvelous job. As founder of Covenant House, a network of shelters for these forgotten children, Ritter knows firsthand the devastating impact of pornography. Testifying as a member of the President's Commission he said, "Of the 12,000 kids under 21 who have come to Covenant House for help, fully 60 percent have been involved in prostitution or pornography."[3]

The number of children sucked into this vicious cesspool is astounding. Robin Lloyd, author of *For Money or Love: Boy Prostitution in America,* documented the involvement of 300,000 boys, aged eight to sixteen, in the pornography/prostitution racket. Is it not reasonable to assume that an equally high and alarming number of girls are involved? Lloyd believes the actual total may exceed one million children nationwide.

Telephone Pornography

It is called substitute sex or Dial-A-Porn. Advertised in many places, including pornographic magazines, these toll calls connect a thrill-seeker with a verbal prostitute whose aim is to please. This booming business racks up over two billion dollars a year and sends the profit rates soaring for many phone companies. The phone rings and Shelly answers breathing heavy, "This is Shelly, would you like to do something kinky with me?" Nationwide, teenagers are calling these numbers to laugh, get turned on, or spice up their Friday evening parties. When twelve-year-old Brian had completed fifty calls, he was motivated to molest four-year-old Becky on the West Coast. The families' joint $10,000,000 law suit is endeavoring to put a stop to such a despicable service.

Pornography at the Movies

Under the guise of "realism" the movie industry has, in one generation, moved from wholesome, essentially innocuous films to an anything-goes mentality. A sizable portion of today's productions are either outright pornography or so-called "soft porn" films (which includes many R-rated movies). How did we get to this libertine stage? Even in the early 1960s, going to the movies was not a risky event. But after cataclysmic social changes, the impact became increasingly noticeable. With President Kennedy's assassination in November, 1963, the post-war American innocence also died. The next year, The Free Speech Movement began at the University of California in Berkeley, unleashing a torrent of negativism. That was followed by the nation's plunge into the morass of Vietnam, a quagmire which claimed not only American lives but its moral fiber as well. The resistance to the war gave birth to the peace movement and consequently the hippie subculture. This movement was characterized by free love, free sex and unrestrained immoral behavior. The film industry began to reflect this "do-your-own-thing" philosophy.

One of the watershed pornographic films of this era was *Deep Throat,* the first porn flick to be viewed by a wide audience. Hailed as a "breakthrough," *Deep Throat* left little to the imagination as it established the new low standard for the thousands of pornographic films to follow in the subsequent years. A federal judge described *Deep Throat* as 62 minutes of one sexual escapade after another. Emphasis in the filming concentrates on exposure of the genitalia, with the gymnastics and gyrations for which porn films are now known. But today *Deep Throat* is old hat, a "classic" pornographic film which celebrates, primarily, heterosexual intercourse. It is tame by comparison with the ultra-kinky porn films shown at "adult" or "art" theaters or rented out by the thousands every day across America. There's something for every twisted desire—sex between men, sex between women, sex between mixed groups, sex with animals, even sex with inanimate objects—imitation organs made of rubber or plastic.

Consider a typical exploitation film showing just off Times Square in New York City. In *The Morbid Snatch* a young girl is captured and imprisoned by two men. She is drugged, imprisoned in a basement, stripped naked and repeatedly subjected to sexual intercourse—not just with men, but also with a lesbian. The sexual scenes comprise nearly the entire movie, and a companion film provides a twenty-minute episode of a woman masturbating.

The Deviant Nature of Pornography

Can it get any worse than this? What about the recent *Hustler* cover photo which showed a nude woman being pushed head first into a meat grinder, coming out at the bottom as ground meat? And what about the inside feature of that same issue, entitled "Good Sex with Retarded Girls" highlighted by the drawing of a man's scrotum pushed up against the ear of a retarded teenager? Or consider the "live pornography" at Club Orgy in New York, where Rita and Victor—"the Fonteyn and Nureyev of public sex"—perform sexual intercourse twice daily before a delighted audience. Sick enough? Would you believe a how-to-do-it rape manual? One porno magazine dared to print step-by-step instructions for male aggressors. Michigan State Police actually arrested one man in the act of raping a woman, with the magazine propped up nearby, turned to the how-to-do-it pictures!

Pornography Affects the Home

The pornographic parade is marching through your streets, too. *U.S. News and World Report* stated: "Adult entertainment no longer is confined to big-city porno districts. The market is moving to better neighborhoods—and even into the family home. The living room is now considered fair game. There hostesses hold parties to peddle erotic paraphernalia, while VCR's and cable stations bring pornography to the family TV."[4]

What can be done about this? The article observes: "Police, prosecutors and others who want to stop the growth of pornography and illicit sex are stymied by a patchwork of laws, constitutional roadblocks and, in many cases, lukewarm support from the public."[5] Make no mistake, innumerable teenagers fill their minds with a wide variety of pornography. In the schools where I have spoken across the nation, it is evident that *Playboy, Penthouse, Hustler* and other magazines are commonplace entertainment for kids. This is true not just in the locker room, but at the parties on Friday and Saturday nights.

The tragic, demented thrills many kids receive from these publications excites the hormones and is contributory to early sexual activity. The focus, of course, is total lust. The female is shined and polished to send the mind spinning in the world of erotica.

The by-product is comparison: when the wife of many years does not fit the build of a "10" she is mentally demoted to less than the best. What shall we say of the faithful wife who develops breast cancer and has to undergo a mastectomy? She doesn't feel like a bunny. However, she is more of a picture of love and character than the photographically coaxed gals of porno fame.

* * *

Where does this all end? Is it liberty and enjoyment? Not at all. Pornography is a problem that assists in the destruction of the family, diminishes the value of women and perverts the consciences of all who partake in it. It is a problem with dire consequences.

5

* * *

Stoned, Smashed, and Senseless

The Problem

Drugs. Sex. In the minds of many teenagers, to say one is to mean the other. In the words of a midwestern junior high school student, "They melt together." One boy shares this story:

It was one of the first big parties of the school year. We all went over to Tammy's house about 8:00 or so. Her mom was walking around talking to everyone. When she'd turn around some of us would pull joints out from underneath the table and take a hit. She never even knew. Later they left and I remember someone turned up the music. It was absolutely blaring—you couldn't even talk inside the house. Later, as it got dark, all the kids got drunker and drunker. There were bottles lying around in the grass. The chick I was with was really wasted and we were under a bush in the backyard and I had my hands in her jeans. She didn't even know what was going on at first. Later I realized I lost my comb and went back with a flashlight to find

59

it. When I came around the bush I stumbled onto Tim and Jennifer. They had their clothes pulled away and were doing it right there. Jennifer was totally drunk. It freaked me out because I had gone to school with both of 'em since kindergarten. Tim just looked up and hissed, "Get outa here," and then just kept doing it to her. It was so weird because I was only in the 7th grade.

There are several problems facing the teenager today. First, drug and alcohol abuse is rampant. United States teenagers have the highest level of illicit drug use of any developed nation in the world. Fifty-five percent of high school seniors in 1984 had used marijuana, sixteen percent used cocaine once or more and ninety-three percent had used alcohol. While the percentage of students who tried marijuana tapered slightly in the last decade cocaine use had almost doubled.[1]

The danger of teenage drug use is not that it occurs, but the intensity of its involvement: "Young people drink less regularly than older people, but tend to consume larger amounts on a specific occasion. The risk of negative results are higher in late adolescence than any other point in the lifespan."

Forty-six percent of Minnesota seniors and forty percent of Colorado seniors report being drunk within the last two weeks of the survey.[2]

Second, drug and alcohol use is not only widespread and reckless it is also an integral factor in the increase of sexual activity. "Jesse reported that sexual intercourse and problem drinking . . . were more common among high school students with early onset of . . . marijuana use . . . . He shows that marijuana use is related to other such behaviors."[3]

Let's listen to the young people.

On my third date with Bruce, I had a little too much wine, and I wasn't as reserved as I might have been ordinarily . . . . After dinner he asked, "What do you want to do now?" I said, "Let's make love." He obliged . . . needless to say, the relationship didn't last and I felt like a slut.[4]

Several women reported that periods of self-described promiscuity coincided with phases of heavy drinking. Cheryl

(40 partners) quit drinking four years ago after a long period of alcohol-induced promiscuity. "The drinking made the sex less powerful. It shut off something in my head. All those voices that shouted don't."

Karen (25 partners) was purposely drunk for sex in her early twenties "because I was overweight and I hated my body and if I were drunk I wasn't self-conscious about being naked."[5]

For one teenager in Lima, Ohio, getting drunk meant his first sexual experience. Since he had never made love to a girl, one can understand his surprise and excitement when a classmate began flirting with him. "You look like Mick Jagger. I really love Mick Jagger," she would say. After weeks of showing little attention to her, he stumbled into her at a party one Friday night. He had been drinking with friends and was completely intoxicated. She ran up to him saying, "Hey, Mick." She had also been drinking. After a few moments of difficult conversation, she said, "My fantasy has always been to do it with Mick Jagger." With that she led him off to a nearby car. He later confessed to being so intoxicated he didn't feel anything at all. He passed out, remembering virtually nothing—no closeness, no orgasm. It was his first sexual experience. He was in the eleventh grade.

Was he a victim of a selfish girl or was he just unlucky enough to have been too drunk to enjoy it? Or was he, in fact, a victim of drugs and alcohol?

Former Dallas Cowboy Thomas "Hollywood" Henderson was sentenced in 1984 to over four years in prison for molesting two teenagers. Henderson put a handgun to the head of a sixteen-year-old girl in a wheelchair and forced her to perform oral sex on him while he fondled her seventeen-year-old friend. These were his comments: "(I want) to pay for my mistake, take my punishment and start life over again. I wouldn't be here at all if it weren't for cocaine and alcohol."[6]

Third, drugs and alcohol have a significant effect on aggressive sexual behavior. The Hite Report records intoxication as an important factor in reported rapes: "Once I was very drunk and forced (her) . . . the next day my mind was very foggy but I apologized and she forgave me for being drunk."[7]

In the following example the victim was the intoxicated party: "I walked in on a woman who was lying on a couch passed out from liquor. I pulled down her pants and _____ her, left, and never mentioned it to her. Rape?"[8]

Fourth, not only does alcohol and drug abuse contribute to sexual activity, but many times illicit sexual activity increases substance abuse. Reschner and Friedman say: "At the root of many adolescent female drug problems lie anxiety, concern, and ignorance . . . about sexuality . . . . We have tried to present a profile of the adolescent female drug user and the combination of forces that may be responsible for her drug-taking."[9]

The Consequences

Mr. and Mrs. Gordon finally agreed to allow Pam, their thirteen-year-old daughter, to have a party at their home one Friday night. Pam warned her parents to lock up the liquor cabinet. The night of the party, Mr. and Mrs. Gordon carefully greeted each guest at the front door, checking to make sure no one was carrying alcohol. Everyone was escorted to the basement where the parents mingled as chaperones among the teenagers.

As the party progressed, Mrs. Gordon was puzzled to see young people frequently leaving and entering the house. Finally, the Gordons' next-door neighbor called complaining that the teenagers were drinking in the front yard. When Mr. Gordon stepped outside, he found the lawn littered with empty bottles and beer cans which had been hidden in the bushes. The guests were ordered inside and told to call their parents. As the flustered hosts continued scolding, a soused thirteen-year-old passed out at their feet.

The party's over. But there will be another one soon, and the kids will drink again. And why shouldn't they? After all, the biggest and best athletes indulge. Why, even lovable Spuds

Mackenzie loves a party. Besides, if you choose the beer that's less filling it can't hurt you.

This is no laughing matter, to be sure. Even preteens by the thousands each year are being treated for alcoholism. America's youth have been suckered by the "booze and babes" philosophy which meshes the pleasures of liquor, drugs and illicit sex. However, this mixture forms a poison with devastating consequences. What begins as simple "fun" at a party too often results in guilt, exploitation, addiction or death.

Guilt

"The first time ever was at a party. I got really drunk and got _____ by the guy. I didn't even know what I was doing."[10]
"I was 16 and he was 21. It was our first date and I was a virgin. We partied until I got really drunk, then he pulled me over in the seat of his truck and _____ me. I really don't remember very much of what it was like. I hate his guts, though."[11]

I couldn't begin to number the teenagers who have told me the same thing. Young men and young women alike confess to being pulled into experiences they were not ready for—because they were doing drugs or drinking alcohol. Many suffer pangs of guilt over sexual encounters they remember only through the haze of a drunken stupor.

A battered self-image plagues those who gave in to sexual advances while stoned—advances they would have resisted if sober. Drugs or alcohol combined with sex produces an overwhelmingly empty, guilt-ridden experience: "Being drunk while having sex is an awful experience that I hope I never go through again. It's awful to have sex and not be able to remember."[12]

Exploitation

Frequently, physical and emotional defenses are lowered so significantly by drugs and alcohol that if a dangerous situation occurs, a teenager will have lost all power of self-protection: "For a long time I used to be heavy into drugs and alcohol. Mostly it was alcohol. I'd go to parties at the beach and get totally trashed. One night after one of those parties I was drunk and got raped. I couldn't do anything."[13]

Addiction

Thousands of teenagers' sexual experiences are marred and twisted because of involvement with drugs or alcohol. A frightful percentage of them suffer even more through the entanglement of addiction. This letter, simple and to the point, clearly addresses the problem:

> Dear Jerry:
>
> Hi. I'm 17 years old and I am pregnant. He lives with his parents and I live with mine. I am writing . . . to ask you to pray for my boyfriend John, that he will quit smoking dope. He says he's not addicted and that he can quit anytime, but I really don't think he can.   Chris

In Houston I poured my heart out in an assembly program attended by more than 1,000 high school students. Afterwards, many teenagers flocked around, firing questions, telling their stories. Finally, only one young man remained. He was tall and muscular. I learned later that he was a star athlete, known by everyone in his school. When we met, he pulled me, without a word, behind a partition and said, "Jerry, I want you to know I'm an alcoholic. As long as I can remember it's been the macho thing to do."

"What?" I replied.

"Y'know, I go out on weekends and get wasted. But I began to realize that when all my friends could put the bottle down—I couldn't."

Alcoholic addiction relentlessly feeds on the mind and the body. Our nation is beset with this problem. Experts tell us, in fact, that the youth of America "have the highest levels of illicit drug involvement to be found in any developing country in the world."[14]

According to the National Clearing House for Alcohol & Drug Information in Maryland, there are 4.6 million young people aged 4–17 with alcohol-related problems. Outwardly, they look no different than other young people. They attend classes, eat in the lunchroom, participate in school activities. But they mask a very serious habit. In many cases, their friends know about the problem: "I had a best friend here before she moved. She never cared much about anything. . . . she was hooked on all kinds of drugs and she got laid all the time—by just about anyone."[15]

Most of the addicts won't admit it, their friends often cover for them, and parents and teachers are usually too out of touch to tell. What goes through the mind of that teenager on graduation night when he steps across the platform, receives his diploma and returns to his seat? What goes through his mind as he rests the diploma on his lap? Does he realize he's graduating—a teenage alcoholic?

Death

When teenagers go to a party or out on a date, someone has to drive. Since most parties and many dates include drugs or alcohol it leads inevitably to drunk driving.

Following an assembly in Houston, a girl rose from her seat and with great difficulty began to make her way toward the front of the auditorium. I couldn't take my eyes off the shiny metal braces she wore. When she sat down on the front row and motioned to me, I went and sat next to her.

"My friends and I used to laugh at straight speakers like you," she said. "Did you notice no one was laughing today, Jerry? They didn't laugh because of what happened to Candy and me."

She proceeded to tell how she and her friend Candy had accepted a ride home from some friends. All of the occupants had been drinking. There was a terrible accident. When the ambulance arrived, all five teenagers were seriously injured. By the time Candy reached the emergency room doors, it was too late.

"Now I walk the halls of the high school, and I walk them alone."

This nightmare is repeated each week in communities large and small. Annually, 10,000 people, aged 6–24 are killed in the United States in alcohol-related accidents. This crisis has now become the leading cause of death in the 15–24 age group.

Guilt, emptiness, addiction and death all combine to present one message: drugs and alcohol mangle bodies, destroy lives and leave young people stoned, smashed and senseless.

6

***

The Rapes of Wrath

When a thirteen-year-old was brought in complaining of stomach problems and vomiting, Dr. Perri Klass began routine testing. When the urine test returned positive, the doctor said, "You're probably not going to want to hear this but . . ." The answer she received was staggering.

"I can get pregnant even if I didn't want him to?"

"Did someone do this to you when you didn't want him to?"

The tears began streaking down the young girl's face as she explained the harrowing ride home with a much older boy. He said her mom had sent him. That was three weeks ago. Now she was pregnant.

The rape kit is a peculiar little container kept in many emergency rooms. A comb and envelope are included for collection of pubic hair and a slide for holding foreign semen. It is a crucial part of gathering evidence after an attack.

* * *

When the police brought in a nine-year-old boy that afternoon, Dr. Klass examined him. The police asked a seemingly endless number of questions to which the boy quietly answered, usually looking to his mother for support. Next, the physical examination began by carefully analyzing the boy's anal and genital area. Using gauze pads which were then sealed in containers, the boy's anal and genital areas were wiped. After his mouth and anus were swabbed with cotton to test for gonorrhea and his groin was combed for foreign pubic hair he was ready to go.[1]

The boy and his friends had been playing in a field when some teenage boys had come and stood silently watching them. After growing nervous, the younger boys began walking home. The nine-year-old was followed and forced behind an empty building. There his face was pushed down in the grass, and he was raped.

The Problem

Rape. It is ugly and violent. It scares most people to think it is possible that they may one day be counted among the victims. However, the most terrifying thing about rape is not how often it occurs but how frequently men think about doing it.

The Hite Report on Male Sexuality records the amazing fact that although most say they would never commit the crime, they think about it. For example: "I have wanted to rape prudish women just to punish them for being so stupid . . ." "I'd like to very much. Not just any woman, but quite a few of the _____ types. I'd love to see them beg and cry."[2]

Another man said this: "I have certainly wanted to. I fantasize following her, putting a gun to her head . . . . In recent months I have become more sympathetic to rapists."[3]

Finally the statement: "I think rape would be exciting and maybe very good sex."[4]

This type of response was very common and the Hite report found that most men felt this way although they insisted they would never really do it. However, there were a significant number who had forced women into sex: "This girl claimed she was a virgin. She was the biggest (tease) I've ever known . . . . Finally one time after much sexual frustration I just pulled her clothes off and _____ her for about 3 minutes . . . ."[5]

And this from a man presently a patient in a state mental hospital: "I recall telling some of the girls I raped: you might as well not fight cause there's no one to help you. I can do anything I want to with you and make you do anything I want you to."[6]

And finally: "Yes, I raped a woman. I did it just for the sex. It was quick and exciting."[7]

For thousands of men, rape is an obsession that fills their minds and a guilt that eats at their past. But for the victim, rape is so much more.

As a woman stepped out onto the street from the south Kansas City law firm where she worked, she was snatched by two men. She toppled to the ground under the weight of one man while the other fumbled through her purse for her keys. She lay contorted on the ground with her face pressed into the asphalt until she was thrown in the back of a car and driven away. After becoming furious that she only had $60, one man climbed over the seat and raped her mercilessly while they continued to drive. She was blindfolded and led into a house where she was told to shower. After this, both men raped her again. After the arrival of a third man she was hauled to the basement where she was forced to perform oral sex. She was led to a bedroom where one of the men assaulted her once more and then demanded that she talk to him to keep him from falling asleep. The next morning, after being raped at gun point, she was blindfolded, given two quarters and led away from the house. Running barefoot down the street, she found a phone and called her husband.[8]

This nightmare is relived hundreds of times each day. According to the U.S. Statistics Department there were 57.1 rapes per 1000 persons in 1976. By 1985 that rate had risen to 87.3 per 1000. Rape increased 37 percent between 1976 and 1985. Can it really be that high? Not really. It is actually much higher.

Victimization surveys generally find that roughly 1/2 the respondents who mention an offense to the interviewer admit they did not report it to the police, generally out of fear of reprisal . . . or distrust of the police. In one study it was estimated that state police recorded about . . . 1/2 of the robberies, assaults and rapes.[9]

The Consequences

It is at this point that rape comes crashing into the life of the teenager. Underreporting of this crime is so common since there is the belief that forced sex occurring on a date is not rape. Psychologist Charlene L. Muehlenhard interviewed over 600 college students and found that 3/4 of the women and over 1/2 of the men experienced sexual aggression on a date. Of this 15 percent of the women and 7 percent of the men said they had sex against the woman's will. The women stated they had known their "rapist" on the average about a year before the ordeal.[10]

Strange as it seems, a study at Cornell University found that although 19 percent of the women were forced to have sex through threats of violence, only 2 percent said they had been raped. Another survey at Washington State University found that "Nineteen percent of the men do not believe forcible rape of a date is definitely rape." Even more amazing, in further study, it was found that twelve percent experienced forced sex more than once.[11]

Rape impacts the life of every person in America. It is a horror that is never forgotten—even if the assailant is your date or boyfriend. The increase in all types of rape is another consequence of the sexual revolution.

7

* * *

Unhappy Hookers

Standing in a doorway along a dark city street, she lets her eyes glide over the faces as they pass.

"Would you like a date? Wanna go to my place?" she coos hundreds of times in the course of the night.

She is tall, slender and conservatively dressed, except for a short skirt. Sleek and beautiful, unlike others, she catches the eye of a strong young man as he slows slightly. Stepping out onto the sidewalk, she takes his arm.

"Where do you go to college?"

"Chapel Hill."

"Wanna date?"

"How much?"

"How much are you willing to pay?"

The conversation drifts off as they wave down a cab. Stepping into a small dark hallway they come to the room. Once inside she says, "What do you want to do?" while slowly beginning to remove her blouse. She approaches and starts to caress him, hoping to persuade him to pay a little more.

"Can't you spend a little more? We'd have more time."

71

Once the price is agreed on, she moves swiftly through the routine in order to be back on the street as soon as possible.

At 6:00 A.M. she meets her man and gives him all the money. He pays the hotel clerk the arranged fee and slips away from her. As she meanders through the waking city in the direction of her apartment, she can think only of falling asleep. She needs to be rested . . . for another night.

The Problem

Prostitution, reputedly the oldest of professions, appears in a shocking variety of manifestations. Lewis Piana, Ph.D., Professor of Human Sexuality at Virginia Commonwealth University, identifies at least eight major circles within which harlots operate. Besides the most familiar varieties—street hookers, brothels, massage parlors and call girls—there is a wide business operating through truck stops, hotels and motels, roadside lounges, residential homes and even college campuses. When a local Providence, R.I. newspaper carried a classified ad which stated

> Indulge yourself . . . experience unparalleled
> pleasure in the form of two Ivy League
> blondes. Generous gentlemen only.

undercover agents finally stepped in.

Several months earlier a student at Brown University had given school officials information that many female students had been coerced into prostitution. Initially, only two students were arrested. However, upon searching one's apartment, police found nude photos of forty-six women, and two minors were discovered.

A professor at Arizona State University was convicted of involvement in a massage parlor partially staffed by university students. Sex for sale networks leer from behind even some of our best educational institutions.[1]

Prostitution is available to virtually anyone in the United

States who merely saves up enough to say hello. With this easy accessibility, how do most men respond? *The Hite Report* indicates that while many men had been with a prostitute, most found it empty, degrading and unsatisfying. However, some felt differently:

> I've had sex with six prostitutes. I felt it worth the money because I didn't have to go through the hassle of taking a girl out and not getting any.[2]
> Most of my experiences in sex since twenty-one have been with prostitutes . . . . It saves the emotional hassle of a relationship that's not working out.[3]

One man said this: "My wife has no knowledge of my visits to the massage parlor. She would not like it . . . I seem to get some thrill and independent feeling from taking these chances."[4]

Just how many prostitutes are there in the United States? For obvious reasons, no one really knows. However, some estimates range as high as 500,000.

> A recent survey found that the average age of a working prostitute was 22; the average age a woman who started working as a prostitute was 17 . . . 63% of prostitutes had run away from home; 80% were victims of sexual abuse; 80% had pimps and 83% had no savings or other financial resources.[5]

How's business? Same as ever. The epidemic of AIDS has done little or nothing to slow it down. An attendant at a casino-hotel in Las Vegas states: "The customers come for gambling and girls like they always did. AIDS hasn't stopped them from coming, but man, you can tell they're afraid of the women. I have one . . . customer, he's still (running) around, saying he'll pay $100 more if a girl is clean."[6]

AIDS, in the rest of the country, is actually helping business in brothels. The owner of the Chicken Ranch, a Nevada house of prostitution, states: "I've concluded that my business has started to accelerate since AIDS. Men feel safer here."[7]

"Reports around the country confirm the pattern in the

midst of the AIDS epidemic. Business is still what it was in most cities . . . except San Francisco and New York."[8]

The phenomenon in those cities is that " . . . a lot of women would like to get out of the business but can't do anything else. They can't even support their pimps anymore, and they are getting their ___ kicked."[9]

Who are visiting prostitutes? The old stereotypes remain intact—the frustrated husband, traveling salesmen, servicemen, those with fetishes. However, prostitutes are seeing more and more a peculiar shift in clientele to ". . . young professionals who don't want to take time away from their budding careers to cultivate serious relationships but who want to let off some sexual tension once a week or so."[10]

Not only is the business strong and the clientele younger, but prostitution has gained a level of respect in society unparalleled before. The last decade has seen two best sellers focused on this subject: *The Happy Hooker* and *The Best Little Whorehouse in Texas*. In fact, the rising status of prostitution is nowhere better exemplified than when Strong Point, Inc. made plans in 1985 to buy Nevada's Mustang Ranch, the largest brothel in the U.S. With this announcement, Strong Point's stock rose from 1 ¾ to 3 ¼. "Who would want to own a sleazy stock and why? Joe Conforte, the brothel owner, says, So they can brag to everybody, "Hey, I've got stock in the biggest whorehouse in the world."[11]

The Consequences

Prostitution diminishes sexual intercourse to merely a physical act. It robs the participants of any companionship and commitment. It makes sex available to the irresponsible, promiscuous and deviant. Teenagers are taught destructive sexual habits.

Society has always suffered from the presence and promotion of prostitution. Allowing it to continue will only increase the negative consequences on this generation of youth.

8

***

Gall in the Family

The Problem

Jenny awakened to the startling presence of her father slipping into her bed. The old metal frame squeaked when he slid next to her. His voice was smooth and low as he whispered, "Sweetheart, I want you to look at something." As seven-year-old Jenny began to sob in fear, her father added, "C'mon now, if anybody ever bothers you, you'll know what it looks like." He pulled the covers back and lay spread-eagled on the bed. His pants were open. Slowly he pushed her tiny hand down as she continued to cry softly.

In the years that followed, Jenny's feelings of terror grew steadily, as her father continued his stealthy visits. Her only defense was to pretend she was sleeping, and even then he kept up his pursuit. Emotionally, Jenny endeavored to bury her trauma. Reaching adulthood, she felt some sense of freedom; but on her wedding night the horrible memories hovered like a vulture and ruined her enjoyment. Today, she admits, the struggle for sanity and the desire to be free from bitterness is an everyday battle.[1]

* * *

It was one of those mercilessly hot summer days in South Carolina when Mandy finally mustered the courage to tell her story. Her pastor listened in stunned silence as she detailed the hidden horror she had endured since the age of five. Every night she would lie in bed wondering if he would come to her again. His presence loomed over her like a monster in the dark. The bed would shift as he sat his 200-pound frame next to her small body. As he pulled up her nightshirt, Mandy would clinch her teeth, close her eyes, and pray that he would hurry and finish his dirty business. Near the end, she would hold her breath in revulsion, fighting the desire to vomit. He would always sigh deeply before leaving. Quickly, Mandy would go to the bathroom to clean herself. For years this scenario was repeated.

Once she had managed to tell the story, Mandy was again gripped with fear. The minister wanted to deal with the problem, but Mandy decided not to say anything else to anyone. Her father had threatened many times to kill her if she ever talked. She retreated again to the silent dread of her thoughts. She is still there.

* * *

For Pamela's mother, every Wednesday night was bowling night. For Pamela, it was an evening of terror. Unfailingly, her father would come to her and say, "Do you want to tickle?" She would always answer, "No," but he would continue. "Well, I want to." She would back away and try to hide as he hissed, "Pamela, come here." Pamela screamed back, "I hate you!" He would respond, "You don't want your brothers to hear, do you?" Inevitably, he would take her forcefully to the bedroom, where he usually stripped her and placed her body stomach down. Lying on top of her, he would simulate sex with his penis between her thighs. Sometimes he tried to penetrate, but she violently resisted. Once satisfied, he would leave without a word. Pamela, disgusted and shamed, would then lock herself in the bathroom and clean up.

Pamela is much older now, but after hundreds of horrible Wednesday nights, she still seethes with hatred.[2]

* * *

Becky is a quiet young lady who lives in a small "Bible Belt" city. She grew up as the youngest of four children and the only girl in the family. As she recounts her story, Becky's mind races back to the first night when she was eleven years old. The image is painful and vivid. Her three older brothers, like panthers, stole across the floor of her bedroom. As she sat up, they pounced on her. Two brothers covered her mouth and held her wrists while the eldest raped her.

Each then took his turn as she gagged and whimpered. At last, they left her; but her suffering had only begun. Several times a month throughout her teenage years, they raped her. Each time, threats were hissed into her ears as she endured the pain. The resulting fear kept her quiet.

One day, Becky could no longer bear her situation. Unwilling to tell her parents or the police, she took an entire bottle of pills. Fortunately, her unconscious body was discovered in time to save her life. While recovering, the story she had knotted up inside her began to unravel. When Becky's counselor broke the news to her parents they were shocked—at her failure to confide in them!

* * *

Annie was about five years old when her mother went away on a trip. It was exciting to get to sleep in Daddy's bed, but she was shocked when he slid his hand into her panties and asked why she wore them since her mother never did. Completely confused and frightened, she remembers wondering what he was doing to her. In succeeding years he kept up his indecencies, often taking Annie aside and rubbing her breasts. Finally, he raped her. She says it was sharp and biting, but the emotional pain surpassed the physical. As the abuse continued, Annie became a "problem child," frequently running away from home. Today, she is a grown woman, but still feels she is running from a frightening environment.[3]

The Consequences

Are these imaginary incidents? No, each is based on documented cases of sexually oriented child abuse. Are these isolated cases? Hardly. The astonishing reality is that hundreds of thousands of American youngsters are being sexually mistreated by their own family members. In countless homes the vicious cycle continues. Deviant desires lead to sexual abuse, which leads to emotional destruction.

The emotional scars of the sexually abused child stay with him or her for years. Sexual abuse ruins the bliss of the wedding night, haunts monogamous marriages, causes teenagers to run away from home, and often begins a pattern that is repeated with the victim becoming the offender.

Is sexual abuse of children preventable? Does not our society scorn such behavior? The answer to these questions is yes. But, the twisted desires that cause the sexual abuse of children are fostered by a society that allows pornography to be unchecked, encourages sexual intercourse outside of marriage and accepts a philosophy of accommodation toward alternative sexual practices. Until these issues are addressed, the sexual abuse of children will continue to be just one more problem fostered by the sexual revolution.

9

***

A Queer Twist

"Hello? Is that you, Geoffrey?"

"Yes?"

"Sorry to wake you, dear, but I just had to call you after last night."

"It was like a dream wasn't it?"

"The dinner was superb and I loved the play. I'm glad you stayed with me."

"Me too."

"What time did you get home?"

"I don't remember, but the sun was coming up."

"We're so bad."

"I know . . . isn't it great?"

"What cologne were you wearing?"

"Paul Sebastian."

"It was fabulous . . . you don't know what it did to me."

"Yes, I do."

"Anyway, I thought maybe we could go to lunch."

"Sure."

"Wonderful. How about 11:30?"

"Sounds great."
"OK, I'll see you then. Love you, Geoffrey."
"I love you, too, Christopher."

The Problem

Like strange twists in a bizarre story, more and more men are finding affection, passion and companionship among their own sex. With leading sociologists estimating that over ten percent of our nation's population is homosexual, this issue becomes important to understand. How does one enter this lifestyle? What is it like to be gay? What do gays do, really? What problems do they face?

The Gay Subculture

The gay scene in America is not a passing fad. Homosexuals form an elaborate, amazingly influential subculture. This is not a momentary aberration. Within our major cities sprawl significant areas and neighborhoods with a strong "inverted" ambience. From the fabled "Boystown" of West Hollywood, California, to Greenwich Village in New York City, gay communities have existed for many years. But the number and social dominance of these areas is increasing dramatically.

In any major U.S. city there are key officials and weighty business leaders who are homosexuals. Why is this? One salient reason is that within gay culture one must be either beautiful or wealthy to truly succeed. As the spectre of age looms over the gay man he sees the haunting shadow of loneliness. Thus there is a unique drive in these men to succeed financially so as to provide desirability and appeal that would otherwise be lost with the fading beauty of youth.·

The Promiscuous Lifestyle of Homosexuals

The gay lifestyle tends to be very promiscuous. Some homosexual writers attribute this to society's failure to accept gays and allow them to form permanent communities. Whatever the reasons, there can be no question that homosexuals participate in a mind-boggling number of dangerous, foreign sexual practices. Homosexuals can get married or they can "trick." Most choose to trick. To "trick" is to have any form of homosexual relation with any consenting gay—known or unknown.

Gays are having sex in a diversity of places. In vans and trucks parked near a bar in California. In private booths at an adult bookstore in Minneapolis. In the balcony of an old movie house in Manhattan. Tonight, underneath trees in the park at Fire Island, New York. And, in New Orleans, gays have sex in public as part of the festivities of Mardi Gras.

A handsome young man in Kansas City says, "A straight person cannot even relate to the kind of life we live. It is not uncommon to make love to whomever you're staying with before breakfast. Then, you trick on your lunch hour. And when you come home at night you get dressed and go hit the bars where it's easiest of all to score."

Gay Meeting Places

Within gay society there are numerous opportunities for gays to meet. On the surface these seem to be the same as those in the straight world—bars, gyms and parties. However, these social settings carry a weightier significance to gay men, for they know that society in general still scorns the thought of homosexuality.

In Los Angeles, according to one gay authority, the rage is pool parties frequented only by those on a special list. The criteria are quite simple: looks and/or money. If one makes such a list, it isn't uncommon to have invitations to three or four head-spinning parties a week. The scene is always the same: an abundance of bronzed males, a cache of drugs and, of course, an orgy room.[1]

In Texas, gay parties are often impressive affairs, attracting men from Dallas and Houston to remote estates. At a recent party, the first floor was filled with dancing men, the second floor was reserved for drug use and food, and the third level was devoted to orgies. That floor seethed in steamy darkness, with mattresses stretched from wall to wall, the motion of copulating bodies competing with the flickering images of porno films on the walls.

Those who do not or cannot frequent gay parties can usually turn a trick at certain bars. Step into the inner room of one such place and you will be hit with the intoxicating heat of hundreds of shirtless men, packed so tightly their sweaty bodies slide against each other in rhythm. The mirrors on all four walls are fogged up. The music surges and drives. It is bizarre, otherworldly. One man comments: "I went home from here last time with a stranger. It was *real* intimate. We _____ for hours. We slept in each other's arms till evening."[2]

In another bar a go-go boy with a tantalizing body strips down to his jock strap, then pulls it off and swings it at the onlookers. A man scampers up from the audience and tries to have sex with the performer, but is so drunk he cannot get an erection. In the back room several men stand on a platform in the dark and watch through a peep window as one man fornicates with another.

Some bars fashion themselves as indoor gay amusement parks. At the Mine Shaft in New York a burlesque ramp stretches across a disco floor. The entire scene glitters with flashing lights and reverberates with a steady beat. But for sex, one must go to the basement. Down there, the fleshy images of porno films illuminate the walls under the eerie glow of black lights. Most of the actors appear to be teenagers. An archway leads to a hall containing cubicles filled with moaning couples. Slings hang from the ceiling, in which men sit and allow themselves to be "fisted"—the unbelievable practice in which one man shoves his fist completely into the anal passage of his gay partner.

Two staircases lead down to even darker rooms. There men shuffle in the darkness. "Suddenly," a gay writer describing the scene says, "the man next to you gropes for you and you do the same. Before long you begin kissing. As you linger on the scent of Vitalis someone else moves close and drops to his knees in front of you. Afterward you move back to the bar to chat with friends. Later, you may decide to return to the basement again."[3]

Jumping Off

A person is not forced to practice homosexuality; he/she chooses to do so. It is not due to genetic makeup. Rather, it is a volitional decision. How does a young man or woman get into the gay scene? One common method is the practice known as "being kept."

Like a man who keeps a mistress, many older homosexual men keep younger lovers. Thousands of youths across America live this life, being compensated for meeting the romantic wishes of their elder counterparts. In some arrangements this is viewed as a straight business deal while others see this set-up as a perfectly acceptable structure for an affectionate relationship. In San Francisco, Los Angeles and New Orleans this practice has been especially popular.

For a young gay man sparkling with physical appeal it is not uncommon to be offered a dozen or so live-in situations per month from older men. Older wealthy men compete for the approval of the new "chickens." One "kept" boy, shortly after moving in with a man, attended a party where he encountered a blither of offers including jewelry, a trip to Egypt and even a ranch in the South.[4]

In New Orleans the relationship between keeper and kept one is termed an "uptown marriage." Typically, many homosexual men will live an apparently normal existence with a wife in suburbia, yet keep a boy down in the Latin Quarter.

The state of "being kept" flourishes as a feeble, twisted substitute for open homosexual marriage, which is still illegal in most states. It attempts to protect the older, less handsome men while providing a means for many youths to jump into the gay world.

The Consequences

The practice of homosexuality affects those who practice it, and the society around it.

Coming Out

For each homosexual who has succeeded in openly living his lifestyle there was a time of "coming out" with the truth to family and friends. For some this is painful, even brutal. With others the experience is almost uneventful. For a few it is celebrated.

Many young men and women, after having built up the courage to address the issue, are met with a barrage of harsh questions and angry responses. Sometimes, the retaliation is violent. The sense of alienation is strong as they are thrown out, misunderstood, or merely left to drown in an ocean of silence.

Not all have such a bleak experience, however. One young man states, "I decided to tell my family. My twin took it well. He told me he loved me for the first and only time. 'If that makes you happy, fine,' he said."[5]

One homosexual California father with four gay sons and two straight sons brags, "Of course my straight sons accept us. Last year I had a birthday party for myself and 100 people, half gay and half straight. My married son and his wife were there, and so were my gay sons and their lovers. Of course, my lover was on hand. It was all very nice."[6]

Another gay man in Texas relates that almost all of the 250 people in his office know he is homosexual and not only accept it but relish it. In fact, he says, during coffee breaks women ask his advice on such things as the finer points of oral sex.[7]

A gay teenager in the Midwest reflects that his parents not only accepted his homosexuality but encouraged it. They brought home to him a 41-year-old man they met on vacation. At first, the youth shied away because his "match" wanted to have sex the first night, but later he gave in and they ended up living together for more than a year.[8]

Some families show to their gay members a weird enthusiasm and compliance. A young man in the Southwest, who openly admitted to his homosexuality, recalls that on a visit to his grandparents, his grandmother let him sleep with his grandfather and the two of them made "passionate, unending love all night." Shortly after this incident, however, the boy attempted suicide.[9]

When gays "come out" the reactions will vary greatly. But there can be little doubt that in America a drastic shift has taken place within the past few years. What was once viewed as strange and intolerable is now seen as merely the expression of individuality, an "alternative lifestyle." If anything, an increasing condemnation has come down on those who decry homosexuality as perverse.

A Burning Flame

A second consequence of homosexuality is the ever increasing need to experiment with new forms of sexual practice. The physical union of the homosexual act isn't all there is to this behavior. There are deep-seated psychological factors also at work which induce the gay man to keep his sexual ardor and need for experiment high.

Two prominent twists are called "fantasy" and "fetish." A hustler in a public bath asks, "Are you into fantasy?" "I am," the young gay responds. "I do five . . . rookie/coach, older brother/younger brother, sailor/slut, slave/master, and father/son."[10]

One man I interviewed told me he was in a Kansas City gay bar when in walked a man dressed in leather, followed by his companion who was on all fours, struggling against a leash and barking like a dog. The "master" would whip and kick the "dog," who merely whimpered for more.

A hustler in New York related that recently he "cruised a john" and was hired by a man who took him home. Upon arriving, he opened a briefcase and pulled out a diaper and pacifier—another example of a fetish fixation. The hustler was not paid until he stretched the businessman over his lap, rubbed talcum powder on his bottom and outfitted him in the diaper. All the while the customer sucked contentedly on his pacifier.[11]

For those into more intense forms of pleasure-seeking there is sado-masochism. San Francisco is a popular haunt for gays into these practices. It has been dubbed "the S/M capital of the world." An assortment of bars like "The Black and Blue," "The Arena," and "Handball Express" have back rooms which cater to the "leather" crowd. Many New York bathhouses sound like the galleys of slave ships with their growled curses, the crack of whips and belts, heavy breathing and crying.

Any detailed and definitive discussion regarding homosexual behavior would be inadequate if it omitted the ultimate homosexual act—i.e. oral-anal sex. Dr. James Dobson describes the deviate scenario inside a gay bathhouse like this:

> If you were to follow a gay man into such an establishment, this is what you would typically observe: For the next hour and a half, that individual would have oral-anal contact with ten to thirty partners, ingesting small amounts of fecal matter from each one; he would have oral-genital sex with five to ten more; he would be penetrated orally by five to ten men and would be the object of oral genital contact by the same number. These men would all swallow fecal matter from one another, passed around from anus to genitalia to mouth to anus, etc. This is no exaggeration or overstatement. According to the second Kinsey Survey conducted in San Francisco, 83 percent of homosexuals report they practice oral-anal sex. The Gay Report, written for and by homosexuals, places the incidence at 89 percent.[12]

A young man who spoke to me in one city said, "Before long you gotta find new things to replace the burned-up old lusts. It's a continual chase and it gets really fast."

Fake Families

A third consequence of homosexuality is the absence of a secure, loving, stable, supportive family. The sense of family is usually missing or maligned.

Gerry is a slumlord and hooker who owns a few houses. As a hustler he runs ads in *The Advocate.* "My lover and I kiss and sleep together sometimes, that's all. Once a week we visit my friend Ann. She's married and has a lover and two kids. We sit in the sun and talk about men. She took a job as a hooker in a massage parlor. I'm part of her family unit. I know all her relatives . . . it's very nice."[13]

There is actually no real family life for gays. They create a hybrid form of family, which tends to breed more insecurity and loneliness. One former homosexual commented that the two most frequent feelings a homosexual faces are loneliness and despair.

It is not surprising that San Francisco, for example, while providing the nation's most open supportive environment for gays, is also plagued with the nation's highest rate of alcoholism and attempted suicide.[14]

* * *

Such an environment is breeding wild abandonment and gross extremes. The question emerges, can such a situation continue without leading to ruin and disaster? And, can there be any limit to what homosexual men are compelled to chase after to satisfy their cravings?

The problems facing the gay community are foreboding. Each is innately self-destructive. Homosexuality is another problem that has resulted from the sexual revolution.

10

* * *

Death by Design /
Death by Accident

The front yard glows with light from the yard lamp as Mom and Dad pull into the drive. The dog is barking in the backyard as they shut the car door. Mom reminds herself of the delicious meal at their friends' house. "I'll have to ask Nancy for that recipe tomorrow."

Inside, Dad goes upstairs to change while she checks the refrigerator to see if there is enough for breakfast. It's then that it occurs to her how unusually quiet the house is.

Normally, Jennifer would be playing the stereo too loud or talking on the phone. Mother shuts the door and goes to check her daughter's room. As she reaches the bedroom door, she pauses just a moment, head slightly tilted to pick up the familiar drone of the TV or Jen's pleasant, happy voice. "How odd," she muses. As she opens the door, she calls her daughter's name like a question, "Jen?"

It is the wall that catches her eye first. A splash of bright red—like some brilliant pop-art painting—covers it. Jenny, dressed in faded blue jeans with an oversized sweater, sits Indian-style on her bed, leaning against the wall. Her head is tilted forward like a discarded puppet's; the back of her skull is missing. Her hands lie across her lap, palms upturned. Between them is her Daddy's .32 caliber revolver. Another life gone.

Death by Design—The Problem

Every day, 1,000 teenagers attempt suicide. Every day, more and more succeed. Suicide has become the second largest killer of young people in our country today. Many times, it is the result of some tangled involvement in sex or some botched-up romance. I have listened countless times to the anguished testimonies of emotionally damaged junior and senior high girls, forever scarred by "good sex" that turned out to be so bad. I've also heard tearful stories from guys who have failed in their sexual exploits and cannot handle the embarrassment. Soured romantic relationships are a major factor in suicide attempts.

Death by Design—The Consequences

Many young people are caught in a web of homosexuality or bi-sexuality and can find no way out. Many teenagers caught in this vicious whirlpool have poured out their hearts to me. Usually, their homosexual affairs begin with a guy masturbating another guy, or a girl caressing another's breasts. More experimentation leads to sexual activity and when that happens, the guilt becomes unrelenting. Many suicide notes document this fact.

* * *

Occasionally, parents come home to find a son dead, his body left in some bizarre, confusing setting. Late in 1984, two New York City parents found their teenage son hanging naked in the bathroom. They discovered semen on the floor. The police reported that the victim died accidentally in sexual experimentation.

Death by Accident—The Problem

Autoerotic Asphyxia. Teenagers have nicknamed this new fad "fantasy" or "ecstasy." An FBI report on a study of 132 autoerotic deaths found that many of the victims had periodically used the technique to heighten orgasm in masturbation. They had always been able to rescue themselves before death occurred—until that one fatal time. One doctor said, "You may do it right forty times, but on the forty-first, you make a wrong move and die."[1]

The FBI estimates that up to 1000 deaths of this nature occur every year in the United States. They say most are misdiagnosed as suicide or homicide or else covered up by the family to avoid the social stigma that surrounds sexually motivated death. According to the Metropolitan Life Insurance Company, some 250 of its policy holders die this way in a twelve-month period.[2]

One twenty-four-year-old man has practiced autoerotic asphyxia for ten years. He began by using pictures in *True Detective* magazine while masturbating around age fourteen. He began to dress in women's clothing he would remove from the laundry hamper. After a couple of months, he became sexually aroused one night while watching a hanging scene in a cowboy movie. He began masturbating while hanging himself. He was most aroused by dressing in soiled women's underwear and hanging himself. He would fantasize about strangling a woman and watching her kick her feet.[3]

One man was found dead in his apartment. He was wearing a brassiere, jockey shorts and black socks. His body was suspended in a doorway by a plastic cord, with his feet touching the ground. Propped up in front of him was a detective magazine cover and two lingerie advertisements. The magazine cover pictured a man strangling a young woman wearing a brassiere.[4]

And they will continue to die. One young man said in a TV interview: "My pleasure is closely connected with fear. I'm afraid of choking. In a state of fear, lust and life are compressed into a narrow space. The more pressure exerted by fear, the greater the pleasure inside."

One fourteen-year-old Houston teen learned of the practice from a copy of *Hustler* magazine. An article contained a step-by-step formula to learn the technique. He followed the magazine's advice and it cost him his life. In the lawsuit that followed, a federal grand jury ruled that the magazine incited the teenager's behavior.[5]

Why? For some, a bizarre, sadistic or masochistic obsession drives them to mingle fear, pain and pleasure in this grisly ritual. For most, it is a thrill-seeking fad that creates a crazy euphoria by combining orgasm with a light-headed sensation stemming from the constriction of blood flow to the brain. Victims are always white, male and usually under 20.

Death by Accident—The Consequences

For teenage boys caught in the pull of self-gratification through lust and masturbation, autoerotic asphyxia may appear like the "next step" to heighten sexual pleasure. Often it proves to be the last one.

11

$$* * *$$

Black Plague
of the '80s

One writer explains it this way. Through perverse sex acts with green monkeys, primitive African tribesmen became infected with a dreadful virus. Their blood was tainted with the dye of death. Ignorantly, the first carriers of this poison passed it on to others through sexual contact. From the interior of Africa it has now spread to every other continent. * Once one is infected, the disease cannot be beaten. It is always fatal, robbing its victims of the power to resist. Relentless and overwhelming, this black plague of the '80s is known as AIDS.

The Problem

Clinically speaking, AIDS—for Acquired Immune Deficiency Syndrome—is a disease which attacks white blood cells, resulting in a breakdown of the immune system. The victim is then exposed to a whole host of illnesses for which he has no defense. The AIDS virus is not as sturdy nor as contagious as many diseases. However, this is little consolation for one who has been stricken. The virus resides in the body fluids: blood, semen, saliva, urine and vaginal secretions. It is passed along by any exchange of these fluids, with the most common being the mixture of semen and blood during homosexual intercourse. The lining of the rectum is so thin it is subject to small tears during sodomy (anal intercourse). These tears combined with the aggressive nature of the sperm in semen allows the virus direct access into the bloodstream. It can be also spread through oral or vaginal sex, if so much as a tiny cut exists in the mouth or vagina.

The U. S. Secretary of Health and Human Services, Dr. Otis Bowen, called AIDS "America's Number One Health Priority." Unlike previous epidemics such as the black plague and the Spanish flu in which at least half the victims were spared from death, AIDS leaves no survivors. This is unquestionably the most horrific medical threat the world has ever confronted. Dr. Bowen stated: "If we can't make progress, we face the dreadful prospect of a world-wide death toll in the tens of millions a decade from now. You haven't read or heard anything yet."[1]

No we haven't. It was only a few years ago—in 1981— that the first cases of AIDS were even diagnosed. In 1987 at least 55,000 persons were known to suffer from the disease. In 1990 this number is expected to rise to a minimum of 250,000, of whom only ten percent will be heterosexuals.[2]

Dr. Jonathan Mann, director of the World Health Organization's AIDS program, warns that the global total of AIDS carriers may reach five to ten million by the early 1990s. Of these individuals, as many as three million may develop the disease.[3] Dr. James Curran of the U. S. Centers for Disease Control states that the current exposure rate realistically means that one of thirty men aged 20 to 50 already has been infected.

One authority on the subject predicts: "By 1991 AIDS will be second only to accidents as a cause of premature death among American men."[4]

To date, 22,000 persons have died of AIDS-related causes. In 1991, when the number of victims tops the quarter of a million mark, the death rate is estimated to reach 179,000. New cases and fatalities from the disease will multiply ten times in the next five years. The cost in medical care for AIDS patients will reach up to 16 *billion* dollars.[5]

Its Impact

What impact is AIDS actually having on our nation? One can say without reservation that it has produced discrimination, paranoia, confusion, even panic. It has changed America.

First, with such large numbers of infected persons, a call for mandatory AIDS testing is becoming a major civil rights concern. The U. S. Attorney General, Ed Meese, recently stated that all prisoners in the federal penitentiaries will undergo AIDS testing (approximately 43,000 inmates).[6] In addition, all new immigrants into the U. S. will be tested at their own expense.[7] Surgeon General Everett Koop is even advising everyone to undergo the testing. These recent actions are provoking legal battles over the question of discrimination.

Second, AIDS has caused blood banks to anguish over the safety of their supplies. Recent reports contend that as many as 4,000 persons have been infected with the AIDS virus from pre-1985 blood transfusions.[8] Doctors doing elective surgery are reluctant to advise patients to have transfusions unless they use their own stored blood. Increasing the problem is that fewer and fewer Americans are giving blood.

Third, the insurance industry has tightened the reins. In some cases, insurance companies are even excluding coverage of AIDS victims with the contention that most who contract the virus could have avoided infection. This is because the average cost from diagnosis to death is around $73,000. A large number of AIDS claims would destroy many companies in the process. Compounding the problem is the fact that many victims lose both their jobs and insurance benefits. The question of who-pays-the-bill will continue to heat up.[9]

Fourth, people are concerned. *USA Today* recently reported that while fifty-five percent of women surveyed believe premarital sex is OK and eighteen percent stated that extramarital sex is also permissible, only forty-seven percent said they have changed their sex habits since the outbreak of AIDS.[10] Many New York gay baths have been shut down and most bathhouses in New Orleans have gone out of business. In one major city, a bathhouse has already been closed while another has adapted to the crisis: tiny rooms that were previously rented for anonymous sex are now used mainly by waiters taking naps.[11]

Fifth, AIDS has generated unprecedented public hysteria and ignorance. Due to a general lack of understanding of what causes AIDS (and due also to confusion among experts on this question), there is increased discrimination and physical persecution in the case of some homosexual and bi-sexual victims.[12] Police officers even wore bright yellow rubber gloves while breaking up an AIDS rally staged in front of the White House.[13]

Many people feel AIDS can be caught anywhere. And very well they might. More than seventy percent of gay men in San Francisco have been infected by the virus as well as fifty percent of IV users in New York. A study in Washington showed that forty-seven percent of the city's prostitutes were infected.[14]

The Consequences

Frank lies in bed and waits to die. He weighs only 93 pounds. His bones just stick out of his body and his eyes are sunken in their dark sockets. Beneath him in bed are towels soaked in sweat while he waits for an occasional visit from a friend bringing food or money. He is thirty-eight years old. While most of his friends are succeeding and drinking up life, he is near the end. He no longer cares. "I look forward to it," he says. "I wish it would happen tomorrow. I have no life."[15]

* * *

Another victim of the plague. The living dead. They wait in clinics, hospitals and half-lit bedrooms. They wait for the end. The impact of our society's preoccupation with reckless and casual sex is excruciating pain. They are the victims of AIDS.

"I feel like someone snatched my life away," said Thomas D'Agosta. "I feel like an 80-year-old man, like I became old overnight." He died when he was 30.[16]

The disease might not be so terrifying were it not so torturous to its victims. The body slowly weakens as the immune system evaporates, allowing every sickness to seep in. Pneumonia, tuberculosis, blindness, muscular disease prey on the vulnerable patient. The survival time is six to twelve months. An occasional sufferer may live for several years before dying —but they all die.[17]

"We're all going to die," says a team leader at an AIDS hospice in San Francisco. Others at the center just lie silently hugging teddy bears and smoking cigarettes. Ed smokes three packs a day. His room is furnished with fresh flowers and a picture of his parents. Ed, like the others, is waiting. He virtually disappears among the covers, his body has now become so shriveled.[18]

When David Morgan began his stay in the hospital, his days would start with shaking and trembling. He would pile blankets high to keep warm. By the afternoon the covers were kicked off, as he sweat with fever: "I really didn't care about anything. I had spent a month running temperatures and literally soaking my bed in night sweats. You just drip. You move from spot to spot on the bed looking for a dry place. You sleep in a pool of sweat."[19]

For many, pneumonia is only the beginning. Blair first developed a nagging cold and then a lump on his neck. Finally he became so ill he was sent home from work. He was diagnosed with AIDS: "I would go to the doctor's office and just fall asleep. I wasn't thinking clearly. I almost died last September."[20]

Tuberculosis crept into his bone marrow, then pneumonia invaded his lungs. He now tries not to think about it. But it's there—preying on what remains: "I could be here for another month or I could be here next year. It's really hard to live with."[21]

For many others the virus goes straight to the brain. What results is the pathetic, cruel wasting away of the central nervous system. Brain functions slip, memory is lost and then insanity follows. Victims suffer blindness, paralysis, depressions and paranoia. Hallucinations are increasingly common among AIDS sufferers.[22]

Dr. James Dilley, director of the AIDS Health Project in San Francisco, states that fully two-thirds of their patients suffer from psychotic behavior. Autopsies of 35-year-old AIDS victims reveal brains more similar to those of 75-year-old people.[23]

Enduring the disease is such a harrowing experience that some are pushed past the limit. In New York a room decorated with flowers held the final meeting of two friends. They shared a bottle of wine, tied their waists together with a scarf, and jumped. The motive was obvious. They chose the 35-story fall to the cement rather than the slow, painful ravages of AIDS.[24]

Entering his sixties, Vernon was a strong, 6 ft., 230-pound rancher in California. He contracted AIDS during a blood transfusion and endured three long years of agony, paralysis and ensuing blindness. His wife found him rummaging through the closet for their pistol. "You don't want to do that," she pleaded. It took only one shot.[25]

We can only be sure of one thing: This black plague of the '80s will get much worse.

* * *

What of the others who receive the virus innocently? What about the children? There are hundreds of them. Many contract disease through the placenta, others upon passing through the birth canal, still others by contact with contaminated needles. Some have even contracted AIDS through being sexually molested by an infected parent.

New York's Albert Einstein College of Medicine has identified certain common characteristics of the AIDS-infected infant. Small heads with boxlike foreheads, flattened noses and wide-set eyes all indicate the lethal problem. Virtually all these infants will develop symptoms within the first six months and be sentenced to extremely abbreviated lives. Most agonize through the last stages of AIDS while in the earliest time of their lives.[27]

Some children contaminated after infancy also fall prey to early death. Cissy is only nine and one-half years old, but she is the size of a six-year-old and walks hesitantly and speaks with difficulty. She is doomed to a slow, painful end which she is only now beginning to understand.[28] Truly the children are the most tragic victims of this new disease.

But regardless of who a person is or how old he is, AIDS is a horrible experience. The virus is killing and torturing more of us each day and it will do the same next year, only twice as many will be struck. And twice as many will die. They will feel like Mark Damen, 27, who said as he was dying: "Come close . . . I'm afraid."[29]

In spite of the threat, America's young people have shown little change in sexual habits since the advent of the epidemic: "A majority know how they can avoid exposure, but poll after poll shows less than one third who are at high risk are doing anything about it. The notable exception is gays."[26]

*   *   *

Public health messages are seldom received enthusiastically and readily; but teenagers are particularly lax in responding to this threat to their very future. Professor Michael Ibraham of the University of North Carolina says: "I have a feeling gay students have changed sexually . . . they are willing to change. But my sense of straight students is that they say, 'It's not my problem.'"[30] The unfortunate fact is that AIDS is everybody's problem.

Part II

* * * * * * * * * * * * * * * * * *

OVERSEXED,
UNDERMINED

The Causes of the
Sexual Revolution

The sexual revolution did not occur in a vacuum. It did not occur by chance. Though it is always difficult to identify the specific causes for the problems covered in Part I, we can make some general statements. In Part II, "Oversexed, Undermined," we identify several factors that have had a causative influence on the problems of the sexual revolution.

12

***

The Downward Slide

One of Angie's classmates told me a depressing story: "I remember how Angie was back in kindergarten—little black patent leather shoes with a pretty bow in her hair. In elementary school I don't remember there ever being a grade card when she didn't make straight A's. She spoke so grown-up about having a career someday. That was then. Man, that seems so long ago.

"I remember looking at her in seventh grade and it dawning on me, 'This is not the same girl.' She had flat, stringy hair, and her eyes smoldered with contempt. In addition, her face was dead—no emotion, no response except this snarling kind of laugh when someone told a dirty joke or mimicked a teacher. Her daily 'uniform' was tight faded jeans and a low-cut blouse. She _____ everyone, or so it seemed. One night at a party she was drunk and collapsed in a closet. Boys would take turns going in and raping her. When it was all over, they joked over where her underwear was hidden. She didn't give a _____, she just laid there on the floor. She was stoned at all the parties and almost always at school. She was a slut and a burnout. One thing for sure, this sure wasn't the chick I grew up with. I think later she dropped out or was sent away. Somebody said she got pregnant. Eventually her family moved away. Big deal anyway, right?"

* * *

Angie's "friend," much less Angie herself, reveals a biting fact about American society: a growing percentage of our population is morally insensitive. Sexual promiscuity in the teenage culture is so rampant, statisticians and researchers can barely keep up with the spiral. The young people, beginning even in the later elementary school years, feel the pressure. In some schools, being a virgin means being a target for ridicule. The sexually uninitiated often lie to hid their purity. Voicing a desire to have a monogamous marriage brings skeptical responses like, "Not me, man!" or "I'm sure not gonna mess up my life by getting married."

This overall lowering of public values has contributed significantly to the rising sexual crises occurring in our country. What caused such a lowering of our nation's moral conscience? "Some sociologists believe that the pressure on teenagers to become sexually active reflects a change in the moral standards of society in general."[1]

It was the acceptance of a philosophy of accommodation. That is giving the OK to any and all types of sexual practice: "'I feel sex is OK,' says one sexually active high school junior, 'as long as you know the consequences, are thoroughly informed, and want to. Then it's your decision.' It's a new generation of open feelings and one of these feelings is sex."[2]

With this attitude in mind it becomes virtually impossible to say anything is wrong as long as it "doesn't hurt anyone."

How is such a principle of accommodation proclaimed? How is such a philosophy encouraged? The sources are numerous and pervasive.

First, there is rock'n'roll music. The medium of entertainment shouts out a philosophy of sex outside of marriage, of sex outside of commitment, of sex outside of reason. For example:

Motley Crue was interviewed by *Hit Parader* and described
this: "We just flew in from Lubbock, Texas . . . Man, there
were some chicks there that were incredible. There was one
who we got in the dressing room, and we were _____ her with
this wine bottle—it was unbelievable."[3]

A later article had this to say: "The other day we had this
chick in the van and she was hanging over the seat naked. She
was doing Nikki on one side and we were shoving a beer bottle
in her on the other side of the seat—it was great."[4]

Second, there is television. From the free love portrayed
in TV soap operas, to TV talk shows, to prime-time television
shows with its heroes showing little sexual restraint. Television
proclaims that sexual freedom is good, normal and to be encouraged. Oprah Winfrey asked one of her guests to tell what it
was like making love to Rock Hudson on a linoleum floor.

Third, there is the print media. From *Playboy* to *Cosmopolitan*, magazines glorify marital infidelity and premarital
sex. Listen to *Cosmopolitan*'s explanation of the stages of a
relationship: "The first is attraction . . . the next phase is intimacy: the first sexual encounter. (Third) a period of intense
happiness and romance . . . The final stage is called 'commitment'."[5] Add to this the fact that Vanessa Williams, Vanna
White and Madonna are paid exorbitant amounts of money to
take their clothes off in front of the camera.

Fourth, in growing numbers public schools are dispensing condoms to teens, without parental knowledge or consent.
We must do it, administrators have told me. Why? Because
teenagers are going to be sexually active anyway, so let's make
it safe for them. This is in place of any teaching of abstinence
or other moral instruction.

This pervasive attitude of accommodating any sexual
activity is forcing us now to accommodate the risk of teen
pregnancy, AIDS and STDs. Many kids have asked me if
anything can really be called "wrong" anymore.

Fifth, the government is increasingly encouraging sexual
tolerance, defending such freedoms as a basic civil right. The
homosexual community has been active in pushing legislation

through the federal government that guarantees their right to practice homosexuality—in the workplace, at public parks and in the home.

* * *

These five sources consistently and regularly proclaim a philosophy of sexual accommodation. The willingness of a growing number of Americans to accept such a philosophy has had a significant effect on the decline in societal morality. The decline in overall moral sensitivity has helped to foster the sexual revolution.

13

***

Is Anybody Home?

"Your Dad and I are getting divorced."

Although Darlene had been listening intently throughout the conversation, these words sent her mind reeling. They reverberated like an echo on canyon walls. *I didn't hear this. I don't want to hear this. This really is not happening. Not to me.* Sure, divorce is a real big problem but not when they've been married twenty-four years and have four kids—four teenage kids. Darlene stared into nothingness as her parents continued their mindlessly positive explanations, drivel about how much better things would be and how nothing would really change drastically.

Twenty-four years. Now after some stupid affair or an unwillingness on the part of one or both to work through some problem—it's over. There was always a 50/50 chance. All through school she felt so good knowing she was in the 50 percent category of those families. Now she was crossing that line, joining all those friends at school whose families had been for years dropping like casualties in some bizarre warfare.

The foundation is gone . . . things will be different now, really different.

"Darlene?"

"Yes, Mom."

"Did you hear me?"

"What?"

"I said we're getting a divorce."

"Yeah, Mom. I heard."

*   *   *

One of every two marriages shipwrecks in divorce. In some places in the United States the figure is even greater. More than one-fourth of American families with children and more than 60 percent of those that are black were headed by a single parent last year.

According to the Census Bureau, this problem has doubled in the last ten years with 20.2 percent of white infants and 74.5 percent of black children being born into a single parent family.[1]

The breakdown of the basic family unit through divorce and parental indifference is the second major cause of the sexual revolution.

Divorce is a messy ordeal, causing confusion and havoc among the family members. A Kansas City divorce lawyer, Jack Cochran, remembers two particular incidents: "I remember a couple arguing for four straight hours about which of them would receive the green clothes hamper . . . . Another couple was awarded joint custody of a parakeet, to be enjoyed . . . at alternating 6-month intervals."[2]

The reality of divorce shears away the fabric of security and trust in any home and it generates hostilities. However, we seldom stop to consider the shattering impact this has on adolescents and their developing lifestyles, particularly their sexuality.

The fragmentation that can occur in a young life is incredible. With Mom and Dad now splitting up, the only real model of love and family is destroyed. Knowing that the commitment and love between a husband and wife is supposed to be the strongest bond in the world only makes things worse when the disintegration begins. What is there to look forward to? Today teenagers have no reason for requiring that love and commitment precede sexual involvement because in one out of two marriages it makes no difference anyway. In fact, the most obvious conclusion is that a deep, loving relationship is an undesirable entanglement, with most preferring simple sexual pleasure and experimentation.

However, kids are still falling in love—that will never change. But their attitudes will never be the same. One young man told his fiancée upon proposing that they had a 50/50 chance. "Is that the best you can do?" "Take it or leave it," he countered.

These facts point to several problems. First, in the single parent family, there is the lack of consistent love and attention from, in most cases, one father. The acute desire for affection from a father can be responsible for many girls seeking the sexual attention of a boy at school. The teenage girl is going through an extraordinary change physically and emotionally and needs the reassurance from her father that she is beautiful and a person worth loving. If her dad is not present or is withdrawn in the home, she will subconsciously turn to whomever is there to get that love and attention.

Another issue stemming from divorce (but which also includes families having both parents) is authority. Who's in charge?

David stayed out late and came home with his girl-friend, stoned. Dave's father met him in the entryway and the shouting began. David, half delirious, screamed and cursed at his father who finally grabbed him by the jacket. David wheeled around, slamming his father into the mirror on the wall. It fell to the floor in slivers. As his Dad hurled David outside and slammed the door he turned to call the police. Returning to the front door, he found his son gouging himself with a broken porchlight, blood streaming from his shredded forearms. "I hate you! I hate your guts!" he spit at the door. His father just stared through the window, waiting for the arrival of the police.

The media have not helped this confrontation in the home with groups like RunDMC shouting, "You've gotta fight for your right to party" or Twisted Sister saying, "We're not gonna take it!"

Third, divorce destroys parental credibility. In the eyes of many teenagers, whether they verbalize it or not, parents are not worth listening to. For many, divorce destroys any credibility a parent has, leaving the teenager bitter and fending for himself or herself.

In the political arena, the irrelevance of parental guidance was further reinforced 27 August 1987 when "A federal appeals court . . . struck down a Minnesota law that required women younger than 18 to . . . notify both parents or to obtain judicial approval before an abortion."

In their decision the Eighth U.S. Court of Appeals made this nebulous analysis: "(It) may do more to fractionalize the family integrity than to preserve it, and may be adverse to the best interests of the pregnant minor."[3]

Fourth, parents have shown an unwillingness to discuss sex with their children. But what are the kids saying about the issue?

> I'm not even sure they know what sex is. They talk about making love and living happily ever after. And as long as they pretend that my life is part of their family tale, our sex talk will be so candy-coated you could serve it to babies in preschool.
> —Debbie, 21

Parents have largely assumed their kids already know, or that the schools take care of it. Parents' familiarity with sex over the years in their marriage blinds them from the intense curiosity hidden by their elementary and junior high age children.

Scott Hughes, a Baylor University senior, summed it up in this way: "Parents should wake up and smell the coffee."[4]

* * *

The result of all this is that young people are getting very little credible, warm advice from parents about sex. Whether it is due to a breakdown in the family unit or a lack of communication due to hostility or just parents' discomfort addressing a subject that was not discussed when they were young themselves. The bottom line is that it is poor parenting. Without being helped by parents through this time of tremendous sexual pressure and confusion, the chances of a young man or woman surviving without becoming a casualty of the sexual revolution are very slim.

14

***

A Supreme Mistake

Janet Roe was upset, furious. She did not want a child, at least not *now*. Yet she was pregnant, with no legal alternatives, no lawful means of dispensing with her unborn, unwanted child. It was 1972, the year of Watergate, Nixon's landslide victory over McGovern, and more bloodshed in Vietnam. Convinced that the Texas law forbidding her to seek an abortion was wrong, Janet Roe filed suit. In 1973 her case made it all the way to the U. S. Supreme Court. The high court's ruling in her favor—legalizing abortion on demand—left opponents reeling in shock. Nevertheless, it was more than the conclusion of one woman's quest. Roe vs. Wade ended a long, sometimes imperceptible change in American values. It enabled the abortion movement to become the third major cause of the sexual revolution.

* * *

The shift became evident in the 1960s through a strange transformation within the American Medical Association. After decades of strong opposition to abortion, the A.M.A.

adopted an equally strong stance *for* abortion. In 1971 the organization endorsed abortions which "served the best interests of the mother."[1]

The emergence of feminism and the Equal Rights Amendment provided a sociopolitical framework for the proabortionists. Under the banner carried by Betty Friedan and others, the cry went forth for "total reproductive freedom" with legalized abortion serving as a "back-up to contraceptive failure."[2]

By 1967 a law was proposed by the American Law Institute legalizing abortion in the event of incest, rape, danger to the mother or major fetal deformity. The following year, the American Civil Liberties Union began pressing the case on abortion with a large number of constitutional lawyers.[3]

Nelson Rockefeller, then governor of New York, signed a law on 1 July 1970, giving physicians the right to perform abortions through the twenty-fourth week of pregnancy. Within six months, eighteen other states had voted into effect similar statutes.[4]

Jarred by the rapidity of these events, opponents of legalized abortion finally recognized the threat. They successfully halted every other proabortion effort in state legislatures. In 1972, the New York state legislature repealed the law which had been adopted two years earlier. Governor Rockefeller, however, vetoed the repeal and thus kept up New York's reputation as the "abortion capital of America."[5]

While the New York battle ensued, Janet Roe filed suit in Texas. A similar lawsuit—Doe vs. Bolton—was argued in the Georgia courts. Roe and Doe were both defeated at the state levels, but the Supreme Court agreed to hear the cases on appeal. The 1973 judgment actually related to both suits, with the Roe vs. Wade decision being most significant. All antiabortion state statutes were declared null and void thus legalizing abortion. One month later the Court agreed to proabortion petitions for federal money to underwrite abortions for the poor and needy. This funding continued until the 1976 passage of the Hyde Amendment which limits federal payments for abortion to those necessary to save the mother's life.

In 1979 there was a further slippage. A Massachusetts law requiring minors to obtain parental approval for abortions was overturned by the Supreme Court. The majority contended that "every minor must have the opportunity—if she so desires—to go directly to a clinic without first consulting or notifying her parents."[6]

As the '70s came to a close, a battle was still being waged over the Hyde Amendment. U. S. District Judge John Dooling of New York declared the act unconstitutional. Fortunately, the Supreme Court ruled (by a majority of one) that the amendment had not violated the Constitution.

While legal arguments ensued, a great tragedy was occurring. Since the fateful Roe vs. Wade decision there have been over 22 million abortions performed in the United States. This tragedy continues today without any indication of decrease: "Every 24 hours more than 3600 unborn American babies are killed. That is 1.32 million per year and it's all perfectly legal."[7]

The abortion clinics are making a killing—physically and financially. Extermination of the unborn has become big business. But what will be the ultimate cost of this travesty? No one can adequately answer that question.

Where is the reason, the logic in the 1973 decision? Carefully weigh the Court's words:

> The right of privacy, whether it be founded on the fourteenth amendment's concept of personal liberty and restriction upon state action, as we feel it is, or, as the District Court determined, in the ninth amendment's reservation of rights to the people, is broad enough to encompass a woman's decision whether or not to terminate her pregnancy.[8]

Now, to apply this judgment in another context: What would the Court say to a mother who, standing on her right of privacy, killed her son in order to free up a bedroom in the house? Clearly such an action would be ludicrous; yet this is no different in essence from the position taken by the justices. While the Court painstakingly tried to identify a principle with which to permit the action, it was never defined whether the action itself was right. Defining the unborn as "potential life" rather than a living being in effect declared the fetus as "less than human and entitled to nothing," according to Curt Young.

The U. S. Senate Subcommittee on Separation of Powers did no better in their 1981 explanation: ". . . the fundamental question concerning the life and humanity of the unborn is twofold . . . . The question of when human life begins—when an individual member of the human race comes into existence—is answered by scientific, factual evidence. Science, however, is not relevant to the second question: science cannot tell us what value to give each human life."[9]

This "logical" viewpoint seems to say: If the mother wants the baby, then it is of value; however, if she is annoyed by its presence, it has no value or importance. Whether the growing child continues to exist hinges on the feelings or even the whims of the person in whom it grows. This is a chilling paradigm for determining an issue of life or death.

* * *

The shift has occurred. Black is now white, white is now black. Since the high court's decision, legalized abortion has fostered the sexual revolution. It gives promiscuous teenagers and adults an easy solution to their "problem." It has given free love and sexual freedom a license. It has cheapened the value of life. It has cheapened the value of commitment. It has encouraged sex outside of marriage. Abortion on demand has been viewed by many as a supreme right in progressive America. Really, it is a supreme mistake.

15

***

Indecent Exposure

What would Walt Disney say about this? That's what I wondered when the movie *Splash* debuted in 1986. As the first Disney film bearing an "R" rating, *Splash* wasn't exactly family fare. I can't help but believe that the famed cartoonist, creator of Mickey and Minnie, Donald and Pluto, would never invest a cent in such trash. In *Splash,* the lead character, played by Tom Hanks, finds a mermaid and takes her home. Throughout the movie they sleep together. At one point the exhausted and amazed Hanks questions whether she's sure she wants to have sex again after having made love on the refrigerator, kitchen counter, etc., etc.

* * *

Wherever you turn—films, magazines, television—the message of sex is blatantly proclaimed. This media-wide focus on sex and eroticism is another contributing cause of the sexual revolution.

Film Industry

Nearly every production company, it seems, is cashing in on hot-sell sex in movies. The film industry is so saturated with this thinking, sex is no longer provocative or shocking. Sex is the expected norm in movies, the absence of which brings disappointment or surprise.

Top Gun, the sizzling story of a young man's ambition to be the best fighter pilot in the Navy, includes the subplot of his affair with an instructor. After having followed her into the ladies' room, Tom Cruise tests the strength of the sink counter, commenting that it was strong enough for them to do it right there. When they finally have sex, it leaves one asking if this is really a PG film. Cruise, one of today's most popular teenage idols, sleeps with his girlfriend in *The Color of Money.* In yet another film, *Risky Business,* he stars in an effort to transform his parents' home into a whorehouse while they are out of town. Cruise, with his cavalier attitude toward sex, represents the vogue in American filmmaking today.

In the 1988 movie, *Casual Sex,* Leah Thompson is an energetic girl looking for love at a health resort. In one provocative scene with a guy she insists that he use a condom prior to their intercourse. At his immediate compliance, she relievingly says, "This is a miracle, for once it is all up to him. No tubes, no jellies . . . I can just sit back and let it happen. I don't have to do anything." Sound shocking? This film is mild compared to what other films display and reveal. Sex sells tickets with or without love. Seemingly gone are the movies like *Love Story* that have a gripping and emotionally moving romantic theme. Today, it is sex without romance. Sex with no context of morality.

The zany *Police Academy* series, now reaping big bucks from a third sequel, includes oral sex. While a police cadet is lecturing, a prostitute hiding in the podium performs fellatio on him as he humorously attempts to continue his speech.

The Money Pit, starring Tom Hanks, is a remake of an

old black and white movie by the same name. However, this time the leading couple are live-in boyfriend and girlfriend rather than the earlier version's husband and wife.

Artistic license? Perhaps cultural relevance?

The high-energy thriller *F/X* begins with special effects genius Rollie Tyler living with his girlfriend, an actress in one of his films. She is murdered early in the movie and the investigator comments on the fact that Tyler is her third live-in boyfriend in the past year. It is all represented as quite normal and acceptable.

In the sci-fi thriller, *The Fly,* the transforming lead character boasts of how long he can have sex now without becoming exhausted.

Every year without fail a barrage of teen summer/sex/party movies assaults the silver screen across America, portraying sex in the most reckless and seductive manner. Films like *Porky's, Porky's II, Bachelor Party, Spring Break* and *Malibu Bikini Shop* all have an abundance of parties, nudity and teenage sex, couched in a comfortably humorous context.

Even Superman finally beds Lois Lane in *Superman II.* The list goes on and on.

Television

Last year 20,000 sex scenes appeared on television. Eighty percent of all allusions to intercourse were between unmarried people. In 1983, the Coalition for Better Television reported that out of 651 implied intercourse scenes, 504 or 78 percent were outside marriage.[1]

According to Planned Parenthood, the average American teenager is watching television more than four hours a day. That's more time than they spend doing anything else in life, except sleeping and going to school. The sex education they get from this electronic parent is a constant barrage of titillating sexual imagery and innuendo.

"Family Ties," starring Michael J. Fox, is one of the most best-loved and most-watched situation comedies on the air.

The 31 August 1983 episode depicted Alex coming home from a date with a college student with whom he had been seduced to bed. Confusion sets in when he discovers the evening was much more meaningful to him than to her. The father's response is to affirm his son's first sexual experience, casually joking about it, and offering counsel so "next time" will not create such emotional entanglement.[2]

The soaps. The word itself conjures up images of lusty heroines and tangled love affairs. James P. Comer, M.D., Professor of Child Psychiatry at Yale's Child Study Center, says that "Perhaps more troublesome—because of their apparent innocence—are the daytime dramas, or 'soaps.' Glamorous people whom pre- and early adolescents can readily identify with, jump into bed—and from bed to bed—often without commitment or marriage."[3]

With the panic created by AIDS some soaps are attempting to portray responsible, "safe" sex. Bridget Dobson, head writer of "Santa Barbara" on NBC would like to see ". . . that notorious nymph, Gina Cadwell . . . whip a condom out of her purse everytime she leaps into bed and say, 'Hold on, put this on. . . .'"[4]

The amount of sex on TV is not decreasing, just the amount of casual sex. This seems to mean only that the characters may know each other a little better or that when they can't wait, a condom will be used.

Another relatively new innovation is the "evening soap." There seems to be slightly more reluctance on the part of the prime time writers to ease up on reckless sexual encounters. Jeff Freilich, co-executive producer of "Falcon Crest," states that no change will occur in their characters. "They have been having sex with each other for so long that if any of them were going to get sick, it would have had to happen three seasons ago. So, in a sense, we have safe sex on our show."

He goes on to state that any attempt to portray safe sex or the virtues of monogamy would undercut the emotional drama that has created the success of the evening soaps.[5]

"Moonlighting" did not need to worry about safe sex after

having allowed Bruce Willis's and Cybill Shepherd's long-term platonic relationship to heat up into a passionate love affair. They took several seasons to get to know each other first. After having arrested the attention of millions through a humorously flirtatious partnership, the show succeeded in bolstering its ratings and making a statement at the same time. One critic suggested theirs might be called a committed sexual relationship since, after all, they work together. Most troublesome in the subtle shift in their relationship is that enough time had passed for viewers to really know and like the characters so that when the affair began, the audience actually wanted them to make love.

Magazine Advertising

In addition to the television and film industry, the magazine advertising industry has recognized the value of sex. Sexually alluring ads are hot market sales techniques to move a product. Instead of direct eroticism, Jovan Musk uses suggestive visual montages to convey its sexual message. A Jordache ad shows a T-shirted hunk with his right leg implanted between a girl's legs pressing body to body to sell their line of Basic jeans. Obsession by Calvin Klein reveals a man drooling down the side of a lady's body. Her towel has fallen off and is barely hanging on at hip level. Another ad for Obsession has a guy and gal with their heads cocked back, their naked bodies engulfed in what looks like the apparent world of erotica.

However, the most conspicuous ads we see are those pushing various kinds of birth control, especially condoms. The emphasis is on "reducing your risks" and the entire condom industry has taken off like a rocket. Over one billion dollars is spent annually on condoms with factories producing an unprecedented one million per day. Different from the past is the fact that now one-third of all condoms are purchased by women.

The female anatomy is draped in every provocative way

imaginable to sell dresses, pantyhose, lotion, shoes, cigarettes, cars and even toothpaste!

The consequences of this one-sided depiction of American sex is impacting more than just the people working in the business. It influences our teenagers. *Time's* cover story, "Children Having Children," notes that counselors and other experts in the field view the portrayal of sex in the media as helping to form teenage attitudes toward sex: "Unwed motherhood may even seem glamorous to impressionable teens. They see Jerry Hall on TV, flinging her hair, talking about having Mick Jagger's second child out of wedlock, and saying what a wonderful life she has. A succession of attractive stars, including Farrah Fawcett and Jessica Lange, have joined Hall in making a trend of extramarital pregnancy.[6]

Jari Whitaker, a registered nurse at Founder's Clinic, who worked with unwed mothers states, "Kids aren't able to sort it out. They're constantly looking for something to pattern themselves after and it doesn't matter if it's good or bad. It's like putting them in a candy store." She says of emphasis on sex in the media: "They say to themselves, *Boy, I'd like to try that.*"[7]

Do young people really pick this up? One sixteen-year-old said it clearly: "There's a lot of sex on TV and in the movies. It's like they're saying sex is universal."[8]

If you listen to the message portrayed on television and film, and in magazine advertising—you would come to a similar conclusion.

16

***

Uncertain Sounds

Debbie Harry of the popular band Blondie divulged this raw summary of her profession: "Rock and Roll is all sex, one hundred percent. Sometimes music can make you come . . . I don't know if people _____ to my music. I hope so."[1]

* * *

Numerous rock groups today are boldly experimenting to find gimmicks and gags which will shock their audiences. Most of this blatant "showmanship" is sexually explicit. In their albums, at their concerts, and in their off-stage behavior, rock'n'roll musicians loudly proclaim—have sex as often as you can get it, with anybody you please. The influence of rock'n'roll music is another contributing cause of the sexual revolution.

Albums

Most rock albums can be judged by their covers. They prominently display body parts, sexual activity and deranged graphics in a fashion that enables you to surmise the musical content inside. But even harmless jacket designs can belie ferociously sexual music. Put that piece of plastic on the turntable and listen carefully. It doesn't take a great intellect to grasp the sexuality in many lyrics.

In "Run to You," Brian Adams belts out the confessions of a man who continues seeing a woman outside his marriage. "Run to You," expresses it's wrong to be unfaithful, but it is so easy making love with you . . . I've made up my mind, I want to feel your touch. I'm going to run into your arms.

In "Boys of Summer" Glen Frey reminisces, reminding his listeners to remember those times of screaming.

Of course, George Michael, previously of Wham, loved the controversy of "I Want Your Sex." The song simply says that now that they are casual friends, he will make no pretense—he wants to have sex. He tells his listeners that not everyone has had it, but everyone should have it. The song ends with Michael yelling out the gritty command, "Have sex with me!" over and over and over.

On his "Controversy" album, Prince says that if you get tired of masturbating, that he will help you. In his song "Sister" he brags that incest is everything he had heard it to be and that his sister has never made love to anyone but him.

In "Sugar Walls" written by Prince, Sheena Easton coos that it is difficult to fight passion when passion is high because the temperature is rising inside her sugar walls.

Concerts

How are these messages communicated on stage? The explicit nature of the message is almost unimaginable. *Rolling Stone* magazine gave the following description of a Madonna concert: "Madonna was a sweaty pinup girl. She wiggled her tummy and shook her _____ . She rolled around on stage and got down on her knees in front of a guitarist . . . what Madonna is really about is sex and there was plenty of that."[2]

Pat Benatar says, "I feel I can perform all night. At times like that, I truly feel like I'm making love to my entire audience . . . Sometimes I look out and I see lust on these teenage boys' faces."[3]

Debra Harry, speaking of her stage show, comments, "I just dance around and shake . . . I wear tight clothes . . . short skirts, try to look hot."[4]

Prince simulates masturbation with the neck of his guitar as well as putting his hand in his pants and shuddering in a fake climax.

Wendi O. Williams appears on stage topless except for strips of tape covering her nipples.

One of the members of WASP struts on stage with a circular sawblade protruding from his groin. Half-naked models are dragged on stage, tied down and simulated sex is portrayed with the band member wearing the bloody sawblade.

Off-Stage Behavior

If all this is just show business, what are these performers like off stage? In many cases, they're worse.

Paul Stanley brags about his collection of Polaroid photos of naked sixteen and seventeen-year-old fans. "That's amazing, that's great. There's nothing like knowing you're helping the youth of America—undress."[5]

Indicative of the long-term existence of this phenomenon, John Lennon described the Beatles' tours as orgies. Roger Daltry of The Who informed his wife, "When you're in a hotel, a pretty young lady makes life unbearable."[6]

The girlfriend of rock guitarist Jim Morrison told *Esquire* he was impotent and demanded bizarre sexual practices. When those did not help, he would become violent and beat or choke her.[7]

Queen's drummer told interviewers he likes "strippers and wild parties with naked women. I'd love to own a whorehouse. What a wonderful way to make a living."[8]

*   *   *

The theme is impossible to miss. It is a strand that runs throughout the albums, the concerts and the private lives of today's most popular rock stars.

Rock'n'roll may not be *all* sex, but it's certainly the main ingredient.

17

***

"I Heard It Through the Grapevine"

Only five of every 100 teenagers say they can talk to their parents about sex.

Seventy-five percent of parents favor sex education in the public schools.[1]

***

These two facts point out a serious problem in America today: parents are failing to educate their children about sex. They are leaving that responsibility to others—usually the public schools. This abandonment of parental responsibility, combined with the humanistic philosophy of the sex education which is taught, is a major cause of the sexual revolution.

What Is Being Taught?

No one seems to be sure. Sex education classes, though nationwide, are not uniform. Sometimes the curriculum is merely anatomical explanations; in other instances it is explicit.

Enter the classroom and what will you discover? What the student receives often depends solely on the instructor. Cheryl Thomas of Planned Parenthood states, "In the majority of schools we go into, there is a lot of superficial education. . . . A lot of these teachers don't feel comfortable . . . they're not trained."[2]

It is important that the parents review the material being taught to their children. Otherwise, their children could be exposed to the following types of information: "Financed by the federal government to the tune of $175,000, a radical course on sex education in California shocked everyone. . . . Believe it or not, it called for the teaching of the details of intercourse to kindergarteners. I have yet to meet a parent who wasn't incensed upon seeing the explicit nature of the material."[3]

"Seventh and eight graders are learning the four philosophies of masturbation: traditional, religious, natural, radical. Instruction states 'Sex is too important to glop up with sentiment. . . . Masturbation cannot hurt you and it will make you feel more relaxed.' Students discuss in class whether they are satisfied with the size of their sex organs. The 7th grader in my city is advised to set for himself a purely personal standard of sexual behavior. No religious views, no community moral standards . . . to deflect him from self-gratification."[4]

The Bankruptcy of Sex Education

For 175 years this nation had no sex education program in its schools. Now, after more than 20 years of such "instruction," the problems of teenage sex, illegitimate pregnancy and abortion have more than doubled.

Sociologist Roger Libby contends that the problems are spreading because too few students are exposed to sex education. This is his way of "discouraging early sex": "The schools should be sex-positive, so young people can experiment in a caring way with self-pleasuring, kissing, and petting. Teachers . . . should suggest waiting until late teens to have sexual intercourse, not for moralistic concerns but to improve the chances for responsible, joyous sex."[5]

He refers to his approval as "non-moralistic."

The obvious problem is that any attempt to separate sexual instruction from morals, leaves us with a distinct moral outlook. To instruct students that they may behave any way they feel is right is in itself a value judgment.

Planned Parenthood's book, *How to Talk with Your Child about Sexuality,* has over 200 pages. However, this book says absolutely nothing about marriage except as an option when confronted with an unwanted pregnancy. The book presents a teenager who is sexually active, outside the framework of marriage, as perfectly acceptable. Parents are encouraged to stick "to the facts" and accommodate their child's sexual activity, heterosexual or homosexual. They are advised not to encumber them with silly moral absolutes but to let them make up their own minds.[6]

The outbreak of AIDS has created an atmosphere perfect for the further expansion of sex education. In March, 1987, the California State Board of Education adopted guidelines for instruction about homosexuality, contraception, abortion and other sexual topics. A task force in Hartford, Connecticut, strongly recommended frank and explicit instruction about sexual activities that can transfer the lethal virus. The Oklahoma House of Representatives voted to require AIDS prevention courses as early as the fifth grade. Even the Surgeon General, Dr. Everett Koop, has called for AIDS precautionary information and the availability of condoms in public schools.[7]

*   *   *

Sex education will continue to fill American classrooms as a frantic, reckless "solution" to the growing teen sex plague. How much it helps or hurts, and how good or bad it is, will continue to be elusive to most parents. As long as most kids have sex and don't talk to their parents about it, and as long as most parents refuse to be informed, the inadequacy of sex education will continue to haunt us.

18

***

Who's "Everybody," and Why Are They Doing It?

"What are you, gay or something?"

"Man, you're the only virgin I've ever met."

"What's wrong with you—you mean you haven't had sex yet?"

* * *

Peer pressure. It can be disastrous. Unless you are an adolescent, you've probably underestimated the grip it has on most young people. Clothing styles, colloquial language and taste in music are all tied up with what's hip in the high schools. Sexual activity is not exempt from this rigorous demand for conformity among teenagers.

More teens are having intercourse and are having it earlier. Peer pressure is playing a major role in this escalation making it a primary cause of the sexual revolution.

Young people are torn between wanting to be accepted, to

"fit," and wanting to be their own individual. This creates an incredible amount of stress, partly explaining why kids pursue sex so vigorously. One teenage girl stated it this way: "Sometimes it's pure peer pressure, but mostly you feel this person is someone you feel comfortable with and someone you care for. Otherwise it's strictly for pleasure."[1]

*   *   *

How is peer pressure exerted on teenagers? First, you are considered an "outsider" and lose popularity if you are not sexually active. It is important to realize that peer pressure originates from a greater number of kids than are actually active. Bluffing and exaggeration are keys to surviving the Popularity Perception Poll. Many students find the pressure unnerving whether or not they decide to have sex.

A seventeen-year-old senior at a city high school says she became sexually active because "everybody was." They'd be talking about what they did on Saturday or Sunday. Plus the guys pressure you; they say things like, "You're the only virgin I ever knew" and "What's wrong with you?"

"Kids are always saying it's all right and you're dumb if you don't do it," says another seventeen-year-old.

"Honestly, the whole thing scares me," says a sixteen-year-old boy, a junior at another city high school. "I think it scares most of the guys . . . but there's so much pressure . . . you know . . . guys will say, 'What's the matter with you?'"[2]

If a young person is struggling with instability at home or lacks self-esteem, he is a prime target for blindly conforming to his friends. Those strong enough to resist are ridiculed and stereotyped as "scared," "square," or "religious fanatics."

Second, you may be labeled a "virgin." Today virginity is scorned rather than valued. A girl who has had numerous experiences no longer runs the risk of being categorized as a slut, although teenagers have their own code of ethics that when violated will result in that label. Sleeping with someone else's boyfriend still incites a holy wrath from anyone close to the situation.

Third, to prove you "fit in," information about sexual experiences must be made public. For instance: "A lot of my boyfriend's friends place a lot of emphasis on sex. Girls talk about it, too, but not as much as boys. One of his friends keeps pestering him about how far he got with me. . . ."[3]

∗ ∗ ∗

Giving in to these types of pressure often means just getting it over, leaving the young boy or girl with guilt, disgust and a meaningless introduction to physical relations: "I knew a 15-yr-old girl who was determined to lose her virginity because all her friends had. She asked her best friend's older brother— a seasoned pro—to do the job. Like he was a mob hitman. One, two, three, it was all over, and she'd lost her virginity, but only in the physical sense. Emotionally, she was still a virgin."[4]

There are innumerable examples of the destruction that is caused by kids following too naively what other kids say. One boy said: "It was definitely peer pressure because there was one girl and more than a couple of guys and I can remember walking away and everybody saying, 'Come back, it's your turn!' I was 14 years old, I mean just starting to develop into a man. And there was nothing. It was so meaningless. I wish I could have it back now, but I can't."[5]

No, he can't. Neither can thousands of teenagers who have thrown away one of the most special possessions they have in order to obtain the approval of their friends.

Part III

* * * * * * * * * * * * * * * *

The Way Out

Is there hope? Is there a way out? In Part III, we discuss several ways for teenagers and adults to avoid many of the terrible consequences of the sexual revolution.

19

***

Getting Back to Basics

Though often mocked and rejected, the moral principles set forth in Scripture are being embraced by growing numbers of teenagers as a solution to the problems of the sexual revolution. In their longing for meaningful, guilt-free lives, young people are turning to God's standards. Many of them have tasted the bitter consequences of breaking God's law. They have seen the Dead End signs and turned back. They have learned that, contrary to common opinion, biblical standards are not arbitrary, puritanical laws; rather, they are logical and consistent, and allow one to experience life to the fullest, while avoiding many of the disastrous consequences of the sexual revolution.

Tim is seventeen years old and has been very sexually active. There is a change in him today: "God's standards have helped me to know that He understands what we're going through. I've always been told premarital sex is wrong but I didn't know why till I read it in the Bible."

Through a commitment to Christ, a new generation of teens like Tim is discovering answers in this sex-crazy world. They're learning that the Bible, instead of merely forbidding premarital sex, presents a wonderful alternative on which to build right relationships.

Eighteen-year-old Larry has had seven partners and numerous sexual experiences. Still he felt an aching emptiness. Today, he sees life from a different perspective: "The principles God set down have helped me because I'm now trying to control my desire for sex. What I mean is that God has shown me other ways to have a meaningful relationship with a girl rather than just sex."

Secular critics claim the Bible prevents anything fun and pleasurable. The truth, of course, is that sex was created by God and He intended it to give great enjoyment. But the Bible makes it crystal clear that sex and the pleasure it brings is intended for marriage only. To abuse God's design is to invite guilt, heartache, untimely pregnancy and disease.

Chris, a sixteen-year-old sophomore from Virginia Beach, has successfully avoided premarital sex to this point. He says it's because of the moral framework in his life provided by belief in God's Word. "It's easier to make the right choices when you know in black and white what is right and what is wrong. Christian principles clarify those distinctions well and if you live by them, it helps a lot."

Simply knowing biblical principles won't necessarily make decisions easier, but this will make choices clearer. More important still than the knowledge of God's standards is the commitment to live by them. Without such a determination, peer pressure and other forces can win out. Fourteen-year-old Brenda told me tearfully how she lost her virginity. "Even though I knew God's standards, I didn't think about them while it was happening. I totally disregarded them! Even now I know that was wrong."

When one is firmly committed to biblical standards, there is an unusual power to do what is right. I have met thousands of teenagers who have experienced the strength to radically change their attitudes and lifestyles by affirming God's principles.

I counseled with one seventeen-year-old girl who had engaged in sex over 100 times with seven partners. Unfulfilled and depressed, she turned to God. Her life was remarkably transformed through the impact of scriptural truth. Sandra told me: "God's standards have helped me to stop making the choices that I had been making in the past. For a while I really slipped into bad decisions and let things go too far, but realizing God's teachings helped me to get things straight."

God's standards for morality provide the underpinning today's young people desperately need. His principles are clear and simple and together form a "safety net" which protects from the disasters of reckless sexual involvement. The Bible provides sensible solutions and alternatives to the jumbled values of our society. Getting back to the Bible means getting back to sanity and clarity so scarce in our day.

20

***

The Virgin Truth

Valerie is a virgin and proud of it. Unfortunately, she's in the minority at her high school, since most of her senior class girlfriends admit to being sexually active and flaunt the fact.

Value Virginity

In today's volatile sexual climate, to remain strong, sensible and pure as Valerie has done takes a special determination. Every day literally thousands of teens are hurried into premature sexual involvement, forever losing one of life's most precious gifts. The person who is serious about saving herself or himself for marriage must be firm and decisive. Purity is to be defended, not sacrificed at the first opportunity. Above all, teenagers must not expect they will have the fortitude to resist sexual temptation. The decision must be made before the lights are out and the passion is hot. Recognizing the great value of sexual purity, and striving to retain it, is a second means of avoiding the consequences of the sexual revolution.

Terri—sixteen and still a virgin—is tough on the subject:

"I think my virginity is very important. And it's essential that the guy I marry be a virgin. I don't want anyone who has been used before. No second-hand sex for me!"

Sound unrealistic? Don't sell Terri short. She understands what most teenagers do not. She knows the decision to wait is hard, but she does it for herself *and* for her future husband. It is a difficult decision that must be carefully cherished during her dating years. The way she sees it, if she's going through the effort of waiting for that one "special" guy, he should have waited for her, too.

Another sophomore who has waited so far states: "I feel personally it would almost be a must to marry a virgin. Something that is saved is much sweeter when waited on."

Virginity's Benefits

In conversations with teenagers following my high school lectures, many have said in varied ways that since sex is pleasurable, to wait is to cheat oneself of exciting experiences. On the contrary, each person who waits until marriage is making an investment that brings high returns. The young man who waits can say, "Honey, I kept myself for you to prove to you how special you are to me. This commitment to love you is the most serious decision I could make." For those who do not wait the real message is, "Well, I did sleep with this one girl I thought I would marry, and then there were some gals I just couldn't say no to. But you're really different—you're special even though I've had it all before you." Somehow it all rings hollow.

The irony I've detected in all this is that most teenagers who are sexually active regret their behavior and wish they had waited. For those who become engaged, there is the painful longing for what might have been: "I said no until a few weeks ago. It was my decision. I thing being a virgin is very important. I may not be anymore, but if I still was a virgin I would sure value it more."

Cori goes to a large high school in Virginia. She lost her virginity to a boyfriend she loved, but who later broke up with her. He's now gone and she is left with the memories of the two times they made love. Listen carefully to her confession: "It would be very special to me to have remained a virgin because sex is something that is beautiful and it should be shared with the man you love and will spend the rest of your life with. It brings both of you closer together."

Giving up one's purity to a person who may be the one— but isn't—is bitter medicine indeed.

Tim is sixteen. He told me he has slept with "a handful" of girls. Looking back he has some important observations— for some they are warnings: "It is important to wait till after you are married to have sex so you can be pure to each other. Then there is no comparison to others and you won't have any reason to want to leave for another lover."

Waiting also avoids so many pitfalls and dangers prevalent in sex among singles. Once the step is taken, it cannot be reversed. For some that step can be a deadly one. Steve, seventeen, has had eight partners: "I think virginity is so special. Once you lose it you can never get it back. One man with one woman for a lifetime eliminates the fear of AIDS and the other sexual diseases."

Are you really missing out if you pass up sex at a party or on a date? If you cash in your investment too early, for too cheap a price, will you really regret it later? After having sex over 100 times in high school with many partners, Kathy has experienced just about everything from extreme pleasure and romance to rape. It is important to understand her feelings now as she looks back: "I really feel it is extremely important for guys and girls alike to stay pure until marriage. Making love is something that was meant to be beautiful and something to wait for. If you become sexually active before marriage, then what is there to look forward to? Sex is a big step and is it all really worth it for a few moments of pleasure?"

* * *

Everyone has the choice: sex and romance now with a myriad of dangers, disappointments and empty experiences, or sex, passion and romance within the security and warmth of a carefully chosen marriage commitment.

What if you're a teenager and you've already given it away? Should you keep experimenting? *No!* Determine that from now on you won't violate yourself again. Prove your wisdom.

One young man remarked to me, "I've made some mistakes but from the time I was seventeen I decided never to have sex like that again. I'm going to wait now until I'm married."

The lesson is clear: Cherish moral purity; it is an investment that multiplies in value.

21

* * *

The Peer Pressure Cooker (How to Say *No*)

Just say No!
To some this may sound too naive, too simplistic. Yet, it works, and once said there's no need to add lengthy explanations. If you as a young person know how you feel about sex and have decided to live by a set of high moral standards, this simple phrase helps you deal with the pressure: Just say No.

Resolve to Remain Sexually Pure

An increasing number of American teenagers are coming into their own, setting sound moral guidelines and adhering to them. This resolve is a third means of avoiding the consequences of the sexual revolution.

There is a strength and confidence among kids who have thwarted the pressure to say "yes" to sex. What a contrast to the regret, frustration and guilt I have dealt with in conversations with hundreds of others who lacked the discipline and determination to protect themselves. Melissa is one who's guarding her purity: "I guess I made my mind up early and I've been trying hard to stay that way. Sure, peer pressure is very hard; but you have to stand up for what you believe. I have been in several bad situations, but you just have to say no."

Decide in Advance

Deciding ahead of time—before the misguiding intensity of a passionate moment—is the key. Teenagers who believe they can handle any situation, or expect their boyfriend or girlfriend to be disciplined, rarely survive. Some young people who feel they are not as attractive as their peers seem more prone to compromise in a tempting situation, apparently thinking they cannot pass up a rare opportunity. Of course, such indiscretion only results in more regret and self-reproach. Determination in advance is essential to success.

I've often been told by teenagers that to say no would threaten their relationships. Girls especially feel they jeopardize the affection of their boyfriends when they deny them sex. The facts remain clear, however, that relationships with earlier sexual contact seldom last as long as those who wait. In addition, most boys have a hidden desire to respect the girl they date and nearly all want to marry a virgin: "I feel that a girl who waits to have sex first with her husband is great. I have a lot of respect for a girl who can flat out just say no."

Avoid Compromise

No matter how noble and right, saying no is still a difficult stance and one that will certainly be tested. Many teenagers today feel they are not loved and accepted at home, so they seek affirmation elsewhere. Consequently, the pressure to compromise to keep a boyfriend or girlfriend seems to some a fair price to pay for their own happiness. Others, though, have recognized this delusion and made an about-face. I spoke with Jennifer, age seventeen, after an assembly at her high school. A lovely girl, she admitted going to bed innumerable times with seven boys since her junior high days. She now says no. "I felt as though if I said no it would hinder my relationship with a particular guy, but now I know that if the guy really cares about me he would not pressure me past my resisting point and if he does, then it is time to say goodbye."

I'm encouraged that more and more teenagers who have experimented with sex are beginning to say no and choosing to wait. A common characteristic among those who say no is an understanding that friends are only "real" friends if they don't push and pressure. The boyfriend who knows his girlfriend has decided to wait and does not try to coerce or persuade her is surely interested in her for more important qualities than sex. Norman has slept with eight girls, but he now says no also: "I think the attitude to have is to do what you know is right and if your friends don't like it—forget them, because they don't have to live with the consequences."

Just Say No—Its Application

Just say no. How does this apply practically in a dating relationship? First, discuss sex and make clear your desire to keep yourself pure. Honesty at this point can prevent future problems. Second, discuss personal standards and promise never to go beyond the limits you agree on as safe and proper. Third, if a situation emerges where you are pressured to have sex—leave. Ask to go home if the other person is driving. It is simple, direct and easily understood. Be careful not to violate personal standards agreed on with a date or it may be mistakenly perceived as a desire to "go all the way" or as a "tease."

Jennifer shared this insight: "I have told the guy I am not his type and to take me home. Saying no is easier than you think."

* * *

These are tough times for teenagers. The pressure to engage in premarital sex can be overwhelming. To survive, a young person must make up his or her mind ahead of time. Untold heartache can be averted by just saying no!

22

***

On Advice of Counsel

From shortwave radios to multibillion-dollar satellite networks, our world is wired for sound. We are the beneficiaries of history's greatest technological advances, able to contact virtually anyone in the entire world from our homes. Yet, with all this gadgetry, there remains a great communication gap—between teenagers and their parents. Particularly when the topic is sex. One high schooler wrote to me: "If I ever brought up the subject of sex my parents would turn blue, gasp, choke and fall on the floor unconscious!"

Perhaps this description is slightly and amusingly dramatized, but I hear such things from young people across North America. In a recorded interview, Roger said: ". . . are you kidding? My parents would freak out if I told them about my sex life."

Justine voiced the almost universal opinion: "There is absolutely no way I could talk to them about sex."

David wasn't any more positive: "My Dad would have a heart attack if he found out."

Talk to Your Parents about Sex

This unfortunate situation is not just common or prevalent, it is nearly unanimous among the kids I meet. Why? Many teenagers have already been sexually involved and in order to talk to Mom and Dad, they fear the exposure of their past experiences. Consequently, few young people ever talk to anyone who can really help them with their struggles and questions about sex.

The decision by a teenager to talk to his or her parents is a fourth means of avoiding the problems of the sexual revolution.

Ideally, parents should be the ones to help their children through these choices. After all, they have raised them and know them better than anyone else. However, the authoritative role parents must exercise over their children is often a roadblock in the teenager's mind. The teen thinks, *I need a friend, an equal, somebody who will really understand.* They can't imagine that person being a mother or father. I've observed that teenagers generally exaggerate their parents' insensitivity and naiveté.

The ones I have encouraged to talk to their parents have reported the amazing discovery that Mom and/or Dad actually listened and made sense! Sure, many parents *are* insensitive; but I contend the majority are a wonderfully open source of wisdom and direction.

At Least Talk to an Adult

What if you are a teenager and you absolutely know that Mom or Dad will not listen? Find someone you can trust—not another teenager, but an adult. Seek the insight and concern you need from your school counselor, a youth worker or minister. These people are professionals, experienced and knowledgeable about the struggles teenagers face. When you are wavering in your decisions, about to give in to pressure, or perhaps already entangled in a situation you regret, you need someone to talk to.

Talk to a Close Friend

A good source of understanding is a close friend. Many young people find their most trustworthy friends to be a sounding board for their own doubts and desires. Shannon told me: "I cannot talk to my parents at all but I can easily talk with my best friend."

Rebecca, 15, has confided in someone: "I do talk to one good friend. She's been in my situation and I can really relate to her. She's always there and I can talk to her."

A word of caution. It is absolutely essential that you act wisely in choosing the friends you will confide in. If they do not encourage you to be faithful to your own standards and direction, they are not truly friends. Little is accomplished by talking with someone who merely soothes your conscience or attempts to talk you out of your commitments.

One girl told me: "I have friends to talk to, but I can't talk to my parents. My friends know I'm a virgin and they respect me for that, so when I come in and say I need to have sex, we talk about it and they end up talking me out of it.

"I talk to my friend who has lost her virginity. She tells me how much she wishes she would have said no."

* * *

Parents, adult professionals, best friends, all provide a much-needed refuge for help and advice during the pressure-cooker years of high school. Be careful never to come to a point where guilt or depression keeps you from talking to these people in your life who can help. If you are under a lot of stress deciding whether or not to have sex, talk to someone first who will help you in the right direction. If you have already stepped over that line, don't wander alone through the consequences. Find good counsel.

23

***

Turn Off before
You Turn On

"Alcohol has had a tremendous effect on me. I've found that when I am drinking it is so much easier to go ahead and have sex with someone than when I'm sober."

These words of eighteen-year-old Michael, a high school senior, echo the confessions I've heard from teenagers across the nation. Drugs and alcohol unquestionably lower one's defenses and break down inhibitions. So, wanting to say no to premarital sex demands saying no to the damaging influence of drugs and alcohol.

Turn Off to Loss of Self-Control

The decision to do so is another means of avoiding the consequences of the sexual revolution. The pressures of society, the media and promiscuous friends at school make the struggle

147

against sexual temptation difficult enough without mixing in the mind-altering effects of chemical abuse.

Thomas, a seventeen-year-old student who has been sexually active, put it this way: "Sex and drugs definitely go hand in hand. People do things on a buzz that they would never think of doing while sober. It also helps to take away the guilt of illicit sex by saying 'I was drunk' or 'I was stoned so I didn't know what I was doing until it was too late.'"

Turn Off to the Side Effects of Drugs

This crisis is so prevalent, I've actually been asked by teenagers, "Are there *any* kids who never do drugs or drink alcohol?" I'm glad I have been able to say "Yes—many kids are refusing." And by doing so they avoid the heartache of some devastating side effects. Thousands more who were into drugs and alcohol have decided to stop and say no from now on. Why? They have found out that drugs and alcohol produce temporary euphoria but they are dead ends with no way out. Many of the students I know see right through the enticing television commercials and the boasting of their peers. They see the garbage drugs leave in their wake.

"I had been doing drugs and alcohol a lot—and for a long time . . . I finally stopped cold turkey," one teenager told me. "It has been three years now. Last weekend I tried to smoke a joint. I felt burnt out and terrible. It made me remember all the horrible things that had happened before. I feel much better now that I'm in control of what goes on in my life. I don't need drugs."

No matter how much is spent to tell America to "head for the mountains" or that "times like these are made . . ." for a certain alcoholic drink, and no matter how enticingly we're informed that Michelob "lights up the night"—no one will ever convince the students I talk to that drinking is all it's made out to be. They know the commercials are lying.

Many of the young people I meet who say no to drinking or drugs found their reason in the ruined lives of their friends. One said, "I say no to drugs *now* because I've been there. I used to get trashed when I was depressed and needed someone to talk to. Now I look at my brother's life and what drugs and alcohol have done to him and I don't want to be like my brother."

Another said, "My sister was hooked on acid and God knows what else. They had to ship her off to some rehabilitation place. I've never touched drugs in my life and I think people who say they control themselves or that they do drugs in 'moderation' are really stupid. Like my sister just went out one day and decided to become an addict! She talked just like they do now."

How tragic it often takes a catastrophe or a ruined life before some see what drugs and booze can really do.

Turn Off to Vulnerability

Smart teenagers are also saying no to drug abuse because they see how vulnerable it makes them: "I feel drugs and sex are related. There have been plenty of times I've been drunk and anyone could have taken advantage of me."

In the gymnasium of a Houston high school, sixteen-year-old Monica told me: "I can easily say no and because of saying no I have been able to keep away from some sexual situations that would have been really bad."

And consider what this college graduate stated about how saying no to drugs helped him as a young man keep to his decisions about sex: "I would go to parties and a lot of girls would be drunk and really come on strong. It was hard sometimes to resist but I did. If I would have been drunk or stoned there would have been no way to say no. Some of my friends have kids now or are all burnt out on their 'experiments' with sex and drugs. I'm as proud of staying pure from drugs and premarital sex as I am of graduating from college."

✻ ✻ ✻

Saying no to drugs and alcohol is a crucial step in the determination to avoid sexual involvement. Although drugs and liquor may offer an intense momentary sense of pleasure or peacefulness, they can be deadly. Their manufactured sensations and artificial serenity soon wear off, leaving the user feeling guilty, depressed and hungry for more. Life is too important, sex is too precious to malign through drug or alcohol abuse. Roger, a bright-faced and energetic high school student told me bluntly: "Life is too short to waste being stoned most of the time"

If you have turned onto drugs—turn off. Before it's too late.

24

***

Thou Shalt Not Kill

Do Not Be Misled

"Abortion was part of my program. We didn't like doing them at first because it had been considered taboo for so long; but, eventually, we were desensitized as we did one after another."[1]

Performing up to sixty abortions a week at $75 apiece, Dr. Joseph Randall was receiving about half of his income from the operation. But he knew something was wrong: "The technology in our evaluation of the fetus had improved. We learned so much more—that it has sensations, sucks its thumb, turns over and has thought processes that can actually be recorded on EEG's. The ultrasound had the single greatest impact on me. There was no way I could see this movement without realizing it was a human being."[2]

After much soul-searching, Dr. Randall began reading the Bible. He discovered a passage in the Old Testament book of Jeremiah in which God told Jeremiah that He knew him before he was conceived. Those words pierced the doctor's heart. His uneasiness grew.

On 23 October 1983 Dr. Randall performed his final abortion and walked out. A short time later he called the Atlanta Care Center, a pregnancy crisis center, telling them his story and expressing his willingness to do everything possible to save the unborn. He now serves on the board at the Center and travels extensively to speak out against abortion.

It took 32,000 abortions before Dr. Randall realized the truth, so he is urging teenagers not to be misled, but to determine beforehand not to have an abortion if they face the issue. Rebecca is one high school student who understands: "Since I've had sex I've had to think about being pregnant. Even though pregnancy would be very bad now, I would not turn to abortion. If I was having sex I would have to face the consequences."

With ever more impressive advances in the field of fetology, we're getting a better look at the unborn child. Increasing numbers of people are seeing the humanness and living nature of the invitro child. Some prenatal operations are becoming almost routine with high success rates. These and other medical strides open windows to the mother's womb, showing vividly that to perform an abortion is to take a life.

Dr. Bernard Nathanson, founder of the influential National Association for the Repeal of Abortion Laws, directed the world's largest abortion clinic. After presiding over 75,000 abortions, Dr. Nathanson realized that unborn infants are in fact living humans who are murdered by abortion. Dr. Nathanson has written the scathing book, *Aborting America,* and he narrated the controversial film, *Silent Scream.* He is one of a growing number of physicians who have rejected the criminal nature of performing abortions. Many of these individuals have come to this position at great financial loss to their practices.

Do Not Deny the Evidence

To disagree that the unborn is a complete living person is to deny the weight of testimony and actual, physical evidence. To agree that the fetus is a human being yet insist on the woman's right to kill it is dangerously similar to what Dachau, Treblinka and other Nazi death camps did. The continuation of human life must never hinge upon the whims and wishes and best-laid plans of the one who carries the child or the others who would be inconvenienced by it.

Teenagers have been very blunt with me on this issue. One girl remarked: "Abortion must seem awfully right when panic sets in. But think about it. . . . Why put the guilt of murder on top of the guilt of a mistake?"

One of her classmates said: "I am thoroughly against abortion. It is murder and there is no way around it."

To a pregnant teenager, though, it can seem like there's no other way out. But there is.

Seek Out Wise Counsel

If you get into this predicament, seek help. Even if parents are difficult or seem distant, finding out you're pregnant is no cause for silence. Many times the lack of trust is exaggerated, so don't begin by assuming your parents will condemn you. Assume, instead, that they want to help you, then begin talking. It has been my experience in most cases that parents are remarkably supportive and strong.

If you are *sure* your parents will not listen, seek out a minister or call a pregnancy crisis hotline. Be aware, however, that some organizations are committed to helping you abort your baby. Politely refuse their efforts and call someone else. If you do not have a supportive family, there are programs available to help you save your baby. Right in my hometown, Kansas City, is the largest home in the world for girls in this situation—a beautiful place called the Lighthouse.

* * *

Premarital teenage sex is a terrible mistake. Unwanted pregnancy can be a nightmare. But the worst of all is abortion. A life is needlessly slaughtered and a void is left that will always cause you to ache with the thought of what might have been. With all my heart I counsel young people to always choose life.

25

* * *

True Love or
True Lust?

Sandy is seventeen, with hair the color of her name. She's a junior in high school who makes good grades and seems well-adjusted. But Sandy's story is far from pleasant. With two years to go until graduation, she considers her life a mess, littered with the wreckage of shattered love affairs. Since she became sexually active at thirteen, Sandy has slept with seven or eight boyfriends in addition to numerous one-time dates.

As her story unfolded, I readily sensed the regret and loneliness in her voice. From her vantage point, the future was gray, clouded by the experiences she knew should not have happened. A wish-it-could-be-different frustration tugged at her heart as she relived the moments with guys whose names she was now trying to forget. Each one carried away a fragment of her heart.

It is over now. The story is finished and there remains

nothing but a bitter taste in her heart. So much given away, so fast.

Then, surprisingly, Sandy smiled and said, "All that's changed now. My boyfriend and I have something really special. We make love regularly and it is so wonderfully romantic. I love him dearly and I know he loves me. Our love is different than all the rest."

After a moment of studied silence I ask, "Really? How long have the two of you dated?"

"Two months."

It amazed me that Sandy didn't hear what she was really saying. Her deepest desire, in spite of (or perhaps because of) the other relationships, is to experience true love. Yet that very desire has blinded her. How quickly she has forgotten the other guys she thought were *the* one for her. The present love is always the true love for a girl like Sandy; but, like the other passions, this one also will go down in flames.

* * *

Throughout the U.S. I meet teenagers who more than anything want to believe there's a love worth looking for. And worth waiting for.

Many have already given up hope. Todd is one of the disillusioned: ". . . half the marriages end in divorce. Who gives a _____ about waiting till marriage to have sex? Chances are it won't work anyway."

Guys like Todd find it easy to scorn the idea of marriage. Often, such embittered attitudes are the result of growing up in a broken home. The inescapable thought with countless teens is: *If Mom and Dad can't get along and stay together, why should I hope for anything better?* One guy told me he'd be better off to stay single and sleep around than be tied to a relationship with a woman he doesn't love.

The majority of teenagers I have counseled cannot define or explain the meaning of love. Rocker, Jon Bon Jovi, made a similar and tragic observation, "It's hard to believe that the majority of teens today are so shallow-minded. Our songs are about lust, not love."[1] No other human experience has been more misunderstood than love, and the ironic part is this: the most definitive and comprehensive set of instructions on this subject has been available in print for more than nineteen centuries. It's part of the Bible from a book called 1 Corinthians.

The New Testament books were originally written in Greek, probably the most explicit language ever conceived. For example, the ancient Greeks used at least four different words for love, whereas the English language just uses one word. I might love baseball, mother, and hot apple pie, but there's a basic difference in how I love them. And here's where the Greeks could be more precise through using multiple terms for various aspects of the same concept.

Here are the four specific terms the Greeks used for love.

Eros.   Physical/Sensual Desires

This particular term is never mentioned per se in Scripture, but it is implied in a number of instances (Ref. Song of Solomon). The term "erotic" is derived from this Greek word.

Storge.   Domestic Affections

A parent's intuitive care for his or her child is storge.

Philia.   Social/Intimate Friendships

Philadelphia means City of Brotherly Love and comes from this term "Phile."

Agape.   Spiritual/Divine Love

Agape is far more than mere attraction or some romantic feeling. This is the absolute maximum form of love possible. Apart from God, humans are incapable of demonstrating this love. In 1 Corinthians 13, verses 4 through 7, an apostle and first-century theologian named Paul gives us fifteen phrases, each one defining a different characteristic of this agape love. I am convinced if young people truly understood the genuine definition of love it would revolutionize their sexual habits and create a desire not to settle for less than the best. The verses I quote below are from the King James Version.

Property No. 1. Love Is Patient

Verse 4, "Charity (or agape love) suffereth long." These two English words, "suffereth long," are a single compound word in the original language meaning "slow to anger" or "patience." This particular term is used in Scripture to refer to persons, not things and circumstances. This is people-patience. It's a slowness to become agitated and angered at another person.

This nonretaliating, nonvengeful patience ran counter to ancient Greek thought. According to Greek culture, patience symbolized human impotence and personal weakness. To the ancient Greeks, impatience represented real strength of character. In fact, Aristotle said, "The great Greek virtue is a refusal to tolerate an insult or injury and a readiness to strike back at any hurt." Impatience with people is still a serious problem. It's still in vogue to tell someone off. It's considered macho to give someone a piece of your mind. Even consumer advocate, David Horowitz, encourages his audience, "Don't be ripped off. Fight back." A Christian counselor has offered this maxim: "What you are is what you are at home." All the facades are torn down at home. And since more than one-third of all homicides are domestic-related, it's obvious there's an epidemic absence of this slowness to anger, even among adolescents: One teenager said, "I try to talk to my boyfriend but he just gets angry with me. Then we usually go out or just have sex."

✱ ✱ ✱

John MacArthur shares how Abraham Lincoln seemed to personify this particular quality. "One of Abraham Lincoln's earliest political enemies was Edwin M. Stanton. He called Lincoln a 'low cunning clown' and 'the original gorilla.' 'It was ridiculous for people to go to Africa to see a gorilla,' he would

say, 'when they could find one easily in Springfield, Illinois.'
Lincoln never responded to the slander, but when, as president, he needed a secretary of war, he chose Stanton. When his incredulous friends asked why, Lincoln replied, 'Because he is the best man.' Years later, as the slain president's body lay in state, Stanton looked into the coffin and said through his tears, 'There lies the greatest ruler of men the world has ever seen.' His animosity was finally broken by Lincoln's long-suffering, nonretaliatory spirit. Patient love won out."[2] A guy who is superpersistent to have sex with his girl as soon as possible illustrates how phony his "love" is.

Property No. 2.   Love Is Kind

Verse 4. "And (Agape Love) is kind." According to Henry Drummond, patience is love passive and kindness is love active. Patience is passive since patience doesn't get aggravated and fight back in anger at pressures from other people. Kindness is more active since kindness does acts of usefulness for other people.

This word kindness comes from a verb in the original language meaning "to bring into use, useful." It's interesting to note that these fifteen properties aren't adjectives, but in the Greek language, they are verbs, action words. Webster defines a verb as any of a class of words expressing action. And so kindness is not a particular disposition, per se, it's a useful deed you do for someone else. Kindness is more than a nice smile; it's serving someone and meeting a particular need. Kindness is never to be enacted for just a select few friends. Jesus even instructed His disciples, "Do good (or be kind) to them that hate you" (Matthew 5:44). Kindness means I would even serve my enemies.

Can you even remember a specific sacrificial and useful act you performed for someone else? When was it? What motivated you to do it? Who did you serve? Examine your relationship with your guy or girl. Does it really reflect this characteristic?

An anonymous author penned these convicting lines.

> I was hungry
> And you formed a humanities club
> And discussed my hunger.
> Thank you.
> I was in prison
> And you crept off quietly
> And prayed for my release.
> I was naked
> And in your mind you debated
> The morality of my appearance.
> I was sick
> And you knelt
> And thanked God for your health.
> I was lonely
> And you left me alone to pray for me.
> You seem so holy,
> So close to God, but
> I'm still very hungry and lonely and cold.
> So where have your prayers gone?
> What does it profit a man
> To page through his book of prayers
> When the rest of the world is
> Crying for his help?

Property No. 3.   Love Is Never Envious

This particular phrase begins eight consecutive negative agape properties. Verse 4. "(Agape Love) envieth not." Envy seems to move in a progressive sense through two basic stages. Stage one is more superficial and is that point where you want what someone else has. This desire to "Keep up with the Joness" is just a socially acceptable form of envy.

Another even more subtle mask for this sin is the "but" technique. For example, "I agree. He's a phenomenal athlete, *but* off the field he's a zero." "Sure, she might have a beautiful face and figure, *but* she's a bimbo."

A second and more serious stage is the point where you want what someone else has to the extent you don't want the other person to have it either. Here's where resentment comes into the picture.

Oscar Wilde shared a fable wherein Satan once was crossing the Libyan Desert, when he met a group of small demons who were trying to tempt a holy hermit. This saintly man had taken his vows, been set apart by the church, said no to almost everything, and had gone into the desert to commune with God. These demons tried him with the seductions of the flesh; they sought to sour his mind with doubts and fears. They told him that all his austerities were nothing at all. Steadfastly, this saintly hermit resisted all their suggestions; this holy man was impeccable.

Then Satan stepped forward and addressing the imps, said, "Your methods are too crude. Permit me for one moment." Going to the hermit, he said, "Have you heard the news? Your brother has just been made bishop of Alexandria."

According to the fable, a scowl of malignant envy clouded the serene face of this holy man. "That," said the devil to his demons, "is the sort of thing I recommend."

If someone else (neighbor, friend, classmate, associate and so on) is more attractive than you, has a higher G.P.A. than you, drives a more expensive car than you, has more friends than you, if someone else gets the position you tried for or is promoted above you, if someone else near you seems to get all the breaks, how do you react? How do you handle all this? Do you sit and sulk? Or steam up on the inside at their success? (Remember, envy comes from a Greek term meaning "to boil.") Is there this inner boiling and emotional agitation at their advantage? Or can you sincerely admire them for their achievements and feel a genuine sense of happiness for them? Are you ever envious? Genuine agape love is this unique and unusual anxiousness to be able to rejoice and be glad at the success of someone else.

Property No. 4.   Love Is Never Boastful

Verse 4. "Charity (Agape Love) vaunteth not itself."

Property No. 5.   Love Is Never Conceited

Verse 4. "(Agape Love) is not puffed up."

These particular phrases should be considered together since they are different aspects of the same basic problem—pride. This first phrase is pride in action. The second and more internal aspect is pride in attitude. The first phrase is pride verbalizing itself through being boastful. The second phrase forms the basis for boasting and is the conceit down inside someone. Boasting is pride in practice; conceit is pride in principle. Boasting is the fruit; conceit is the root.

"(Agape) vaunteth not itself." In the original language, this term for vaunteth means literally "a bag of wind, a windbag, a bunch of hot air." Paul has in mind a braggart, a big talker, a blow-hard, someone shooting off his mouth about himself.

Typically, boastful people don't seem to be the endearing types. No one likes to be around someone who brags for one simple reason: bragging is either an intentional or unintentional effort to make someone else feel inferior to you. It's geared to make you look good and them not so good. Bona fide love would never brag or boast since agape love doesn't strut around feeling and acting superior.

"(Agape Love) is not puffed up." This term for puffed up is a metaphor meaning to be inflated with pride. Conceit is someone's inflationary perspective on himself, where he has a higher opinion of himself than he should. Agape Love is never conceited. Since any good someone has or is comes from God Himself, there is no reason or room for any conceit. Being humble is realizing who you are, realizing Who made you who you are, and giving God the credit for it all. Conceit is bigheaded, Agape is big-hearted.

Property No. 6.   Love Is Never Inconsiderate

Verse 5. "(Agape Love) doth not behave itself unseemly." This Greek verb for "unseemly" might better be translated "inconsiderate." Agape Love doesn't behave in an unbecoming or inconsiderate manner. It's never impolite or degrading, never disrespectful, never thoughtless, coarse, crude, or rude. Southern California has made infamous a vernacular form called "Valley Talk." Phrases like "Gag on a maggot" and "Barf out" are the antitheses of this particular agape love characteristic.

According to experts, 80 percent of all communication is nonverbal. Even body language, i.e. posture, gestures, and facial expressions, can be construed by others as being inconsiderate.

Remember, the primary problem behind any inconsiderate behavior is this carelessness about anyone else's feelings or sensitivities. Rudeness can't possibly love since rudeness is an absolute disregard for what affects someone else.

Property No. 7.   Love Is Never Selfish

Verse 5. "(Agape Love) seeketh not her own." Agape is not primarily interested in itself; it is much more interested in someone else. In contrast, consider these examples from the "Me Generation."

"I know I am really in love with my boyfriend, because I couldn't live without him. I'd die."

"I know my boyfriend really loves me 'cause he's really jealous of other guys. He beat me once because of it, but I know he didn't mean to."

For these teenagers, the hidden agenda behind "I love you" is really "I love me and I want you"–selfishness.

A confused woman confessed to her counselor, "There's a gentleman I'm seeing who says he loves me so much he will commit suicide if I don't marry him. What should I do?"

"Stop seeing him," said the counselor, "This man doesn't love you. He loves himself. Suicide is the ultimate act of selfishness."

Mae Hobson knows firsthand the horrible and even irreversible consequences of selfishness. Her nine-year-old daughter, Nicole, began having convulsions on a Chicago city bus.

Another passenger acting as a good Samaritan came to her aid when the bus driver refused to leave his route. "The woman was sitting there screaming her baby was having a heart attack, she's got a pacemaker, and the bus driver was telling her, 'Get off the (blankety-blank) bus, lady,'" said Ted Garrettson, identified by a hospital spokesman as the man who carried Nicole Hobson into the emergency room.

"I asked the bus driver, would he keep going straight a block to the hospital? He said he couldn't do it, he had to turn there," said Mae Hobson, 40, Nicole's mother.

"And a gentleman from the back of the bus came up and offered his service and he took my little girl and we ran about a block to the hospital." The tragic part is Nicole died in the emergency room, and chances are she would still be alive if a stubborn bus driver had cared enough to set aside high self-centeredness and driven on one more block to the hospital.

Property No. 8.   Love Is Never Provoked

Verse 5. "(Agape Love) is not easily provoked." Provoked implies "a sudden outburst of anger," meaning agape is never short tempered. Agape guards against being irritable and annoyed—against being easily ruffled and edgy. No one has to tiptoe on eggshells around agape. Agape-possessed people don't resemble a short-fused piece of dynamite. This particular agape aspect is either demonstrated or denied at flight delays, in crowded restaurants, in long grocery lines, or in rush hour bumper-to-bumper traffic.

How many guys are like a "time-bomb" ready to go off at their girlfriend over the slightest offense? Again, this virtue reveals so clearly how artificial their "love" really is.

Property No. 9.   Love Never Remembers a Personal Offense

Verse 5. "(Agape Love) thinketh no evil." In the Greek language this phrase, "thinketh no evil," is the word *"logizo-mai." Logizomai* was a word an ancient accountant would use, a bookkeeper's term. It meant to keep a mathematical account. *Logizomai* is a word that was used for entering the amount of an item into a ledger so that it would not be forgotten. This *logizomai* was a running record of what someone owed you or what you owed them. But Paul said agape love is not *logizomai,* meaning love does not keep books on all the bad which has been done to it. Love never keeps this running record of offenses which have been committed against it.

In simplistic language, agape love forgives and then forgets. This doesn't mean the actual offense is forever erased from the mind. Total amnesia is neither desirable nor attainable. Forgetting a personal offense means refusing to be resentful and bitter at the sin committed against one. This particular aspect is never vindictive or hateful. It does not harbor grudges, never holding someone accountable for a previous wrong or injury.

Bob and Goldie Bristol from Dearborn, Michigan, drove more than 2,000 miles to speak to a group of some sixty inmates in the prison chapel at the California Men's Colony, San Luis Obispo, California. Their mission brought them to see their "special person," prisoner Michael Keeyes. Michael had murdered their daughter, Diane, age twenty, in San Diego's North Park area. She had been selling encyclopedias door to door when she was accosted, raped and strangled. The San Diego judge who sentenced Keeyes to life imprisonment said he was "cunning, calculating, and callous, the most vicious killer I have encountered in my life."

The Bristols are a Christian couple and realize the state has a God-given responsibility to punish Mr. Keeyes. But on a personal basis they are forgiving him for committing this hideous act against their daughter. Mrs. Bristol said, "We harbor no hatred, no revenge, and what would make us the happiest is when Michael accepts Jesus Christ."

Keeyes, who at first admitted to the Bristols that he didn't quite understand their act, told his fellow inmates that people like the Bristols give meaning to the word "forgiveness."

Agape forgives and forgets and if someone else does recall a previous offense, it still forgives.

Property No. 10.   Love Never Rejoices in Unrighteousness

Verse 6. "(Agape Love) rejoiceth not in iniquity" (here iniquity is a synonym for sin or unrighteousness). This particular characteristic could be broken down into two basic parts.

First, agape love never rejoices in someone's own sin. Locker rooms, barber shops, and even socializing around the office coffeepot offer opportunities for sharing sensationalized, sordid and sinful details. Remember, any sexual behavior outside monogamous heterosexual marriage grieves God; how then is it possible to love Him and still feel good and be glad in doing the very things that so offend Him?

Second, agape love never rejoices in someone else's sin. Rejoicing in another's sin is the smugness and satisfaction some people feel when someone else commits a particular and more obvious sin. There's this secret gladness if someone else messes up so that they can look better; and if there are ensuing consequences from this sin, others might hide behind a sanctimonious veneer and comment, "He's just getting what he deserves."

Actually, this particular sin forms the basis for gossip, since in essence, gossip gloats and is glad at the problems and imperfections in others. And remember, gossip is still gossip even if it's true. It's how something true is shared and often it's the fact it is shared that makes gossip gossip.

Potentially, there is a threefold harm in gossip. One, gossip harms the one who gossips; second, gossip harms the one who hears the gossip; and third, gossip can do irreparable harm to the one gossiped about.

A fable is told of a man who shared some information about a friend, only to find out later that what he had said was not completely accurate. Troubled in his conscience, he went to a wise man to seek advice. This wise man said to him, "If you want to make peace with your conscience, you must fill a bag with feathers and go to every dooryard in the village and drop each of them one feather."

The man did as he was told, and returning to the village wise man, announced that he had done penance for his sins.

"Not yet," said the wise man sternly. "Take up your bag, go the rounds again, and gather up every feather that you have dropped."

"But," exclaimed the man, "the wind has blown them all away by this time. I cannot pick them all up again."

"Yes," answered the village wise man, "and so it is with gossip. Words are easily dropped, but no matter how hard you try, you can never pick them back up again."

Agape never gossips since agape could never rejoice in someone else's unrighteousness.

Property No. 11.   Love Rejoices in Truthfulness

Verse 6. "(Agape Love) rejoiceth in truth." After commenting on eight negatives, things that love isn't or doesn't do, Paul mentions five more positive aspects.

Rejoicing in truthfulness means to be enthusiastic, encouraged, and on occasion even ecstatic at both seeing and hearing truthfulness in and from someone else. Unfortunately, our culture has continued to de-emphasize moral and ethical values.

* A study accuses 47 Harvard and Emory University scientists of producing misleading papers.
* A congressional subcommittee estimates that one of every three Americans falsifies career or educational credentials to get jobs.
* Vicious "negative campaigning" in recent elections was fueled by deliberate misinformation about opponents.
* A. U.S. News Cable Network poll revealed that only 49 percent of those asked believe their ministers are always truthful about serious subjects.

*   This rampant disregard for truthfulness has encouraged one New York City school teacher *not* to praise a student who turned in a purse she found containing $1,000.00. How sad. Genuine agape rejoices in and even rewards integrity.[3]

Property No. 12.   Love Bears All Things

Verse 7. "(Agape Love) beareth all things." This particular phrase means "to protect or to cover." Solomon said it this way, "Hatred stirreth up strife, but *love covereth all sin*" (Proverbs 10:12). This doesn't mean to sweep sin under the carpet a la Watergate, but it does mean not to expose someone's sin unnecessarily. If there's ugliness in someone else's life, the normal human reaction is to hang their dirty laundry out for everyone to see; but real love tries to keep private sin private and correct the problem with the least possible hurt and harm to the guilty party. Love is hesitant to drag a scandal in front of anyone. Love bears, it doesn't bare.

Property No. 13.   Love Believes All Things

Verse 7. "(Agape Love) believeth all things." This phrase can't possibly imply getting rid of good sense and being gullible or naive; it doesn't mean you just fall for anything and, in an undiscerning manner, believe whatever someone tells you. "Believeth all things" just means love is never cynical or suspicious, never jumping to premature conclusions, never anxious to believe a rumor or wrong in someone else.

Love subscribes to the judicial principle, "Someone is considered innocent until proven guilty." Love wants to believe the best in someone. If you're going to make a mistake about someone, then err on the side of agape. It would be far better if you took a chance on a person and believed in him too much than refuse to believe in him at all. Even if there's a reasonable possibility a person might mess up, if you can still believe in him, it can often exert a positive influence that will make people want to do their best never to let you down.

Property No. 14. Love Hopes All Things

Verse 7. "(Agape Love) hopeth all things." This means love is optimistic. Through agape, disillusioned teenagers can still hope for a fulfilling marriage. Through agape, parents of a rebellious child can hope for a cure to his seeming incorrigibility. Through agape, the spouse of an unfaithful mate can continue to hope for a reconciliation. Love doesn't give up on anyone. Because love believes failure is never final, love hangs on and continues to hope even against hope.

Property No. 15. Love Endures All Things

Verse 7. "(Agape Love) endureth all things." Ancient military strategists used this term to denote an army's holding a vital position at any cost. This means love can wait for marriage and can endure hardship, temptation, or any of the typical problems associated with this waiting. Lust requires sex in order to continue; true love endures at any cost and waits and waits. In virtually every case, teenagers I meet are focusing on romance, companionship and unrestrained passion instead of love, never realizing anything besides genuine love will fade and eventually be forgotten. True love, agape, never ends.

* * *

Remember, success in any relationship (friendship, marriage, and so on) involves more than finding the right person, it's *being* the right person. And it's virtually impossible to be the person you should be apart from this love.

Thus, the critical question is how do you stack up against these fifteen characteristics? For example, kindness is people-patience plus one more step. Kindness not only endures the offenses of others (patience), but even strives to meet the offender's needs. Remember, kindness literally means "to be useful." Are you useful to others, even to those who offend you? When someone is angry or antagonistic toward you, is your first reaction to do something kind for them? Would others around you sincerely characterize you as being a kind person? And so the issue remains, are these properties an integral part of you? Is each one of these qualities incarnate in you?

These particular phrases characterize agape love, and no matter who you are, this ultimate love form from God cannot be experienced apart from a personal relationship with His Son, Jesus Christ. True love can be yours, and if you want to know how, then please read the final chapter of this book.

Love is not merely an emotion. It is a commitment to meet the needs of another without regard to what is received in return. Love demands a choice and is better expressed in actions than felt in the emotions. The feelings teens so often associate with love are usually infatuation or even self-serving affection.

Some of the most sexually active kids I meet are the first to confess that they have never *really* been in love. If one has a long string of sexual partners, usually there is denial that true love existed in any except the present relationship. Though missing the illogicality of their behavior, these kids tell me they know true love never ends. Yet they continue moving from "true love" to "true love."

True love is patient and respects others. There is never any pressure to lower another's standards or maneuvering to "go all the way." True love waits—it doesn't require sex to continue. True love admires and builds up the other person. It is a fortress of strength and security which helps the other be better instead of worse and pulled down into guilt. True love is sensitive to the other person first. Communication is open, warm and unselfish.

True love means unconditional commitment, accepting without strings attached. However, it also expects the best in the other.

True love is righteous. It never compromises morals in order to continue existing. It never violates the conscience because of the excuse that "We love each other *so* much." It exists hand in hand with the wholesomeness of respect and goodness.

In virtually every case, teenagers I meet are focusing on romance, companionship and passion rather than true love. Yet anything besides genuine love will fade and eventually be forgotten. True love—which is also true friendship—never ends. Being in love also means understanding that directions may change and marriage may not lie ahead. That's why it patiently waits. Contrast that with the following:

I know I've never really been in love and I'm not sure what it is.

∗ ∗ ∗

Love is when you feel really good about another and you want to be with them forever.

∗ ∗ ∗

I'm not real sure what love is. I think real love is essential for sex to mean something. We have sex and it means something.

∗ ∗ ∗

I made love to this girlfriend and I never felt closer to anyone in the world. She's more than just a girl friend.

Do you see the common malady in these statements? These teenagers have "I" trouble. They are thinking about themselves, their desires, their drives. In all likelihood, true love is absent in every one of these individuals.

Teenagers: Wait until you understand the maturity, self-control and commitment involved in true love. These are the elements of the only foundation on which a relationship can be built to survive.

26

***

How to Live
Happily Ever After

Is it really possible to find love and live happily ever after? Yes. And, as you might imagine, the key to this kind of fulfilling life is a special Someone—a Person whose understanding and compassion are without equal. There is such a Person, of course. He knows more about you than your parents or your friends. He even knows you better than you know yourself—in fact, He created you. Yes, God—your Creator—is the key to your discovery of true and lasting happiness.

As an intelligent individual you realize that your life, with all its complexity, was not the result of a biological accident. The Designer and Maker of your body and soul knows you perfectly; and because He made you He also knows what is best for you and essential to your happiness.

So, how are you and God getting along? Are you relating? Communicating? Let's be honest: Do you *really* feel you even know Him? In American society, openly relating to God isn't exactly commonplace. Oh, we may hear a movie star give Him thanks for helping out with an Oscar-winning performance, or Dad may actually pray over Thanksgiving dinner; but most people ignore God on a daily basis. Religion still enjoys a measure of popularity, yet, for the majority it may be more a way of appeasing God than really knowing Him.

Why aren't too many of us getting along well with God? Perhaps it's because we fear that relating to Him fully and doing His will would really mess up our plans. What's more, we can't help but think that He's there, leaning over the balcony of heaven, just waiting for us to enjoy ourselves so He can yell, "Cut that out!" Some of us feel He is too vague and far away to know anyway. Is God too vague? Is He knowable? What has He done to make possible an encounter with Him (since millions of people on Planet Earth claim to have had one)?

First, God has revealed Himself through His Word, the Bible. In the pages of this Book God records His dealings with people throughout history. He also tells us what He is like and how we can have a relationship with Him. Interestingly, the Bible tells us about ourselves, too.

The Bible states that all men are sinful and have rebelled against God. Romans 3:23 says that "all have sinned and fall short of the glory of God." To many of us, this is an obvious truth. We know when we have turned our backs on God and His will and gone our own way instead. We know what it means to be in control of our own lives, caring little about wrong or right.

Our sinfulness is a barrier, separating us from God and breaking our ability to know Him and have fellowship with Him. We are not robots. God has created us with the freedom to choose how we will live. In fact, the greatest power He has entrusted to us is the power of choice. However, there are severe, even deadly consequences to making the wrong choices when it comes to spiritual matters. Romans 6:23 warns, "the wages of sin is death . . . ."

We are eternal beings. Our bodies only last a few years before they wear out and die, but there is an immaterial part of our being that will exist eternally somewhere. Either you will live forever in heaven in God's perfect peace and care—or forever in hell. Whether you spend eternity in heaven or hell depends on the way you exercise that power of choice God has given you.

Our sin has created a chasm so great we cannot do anything to earn our way back into God's fellowship. The gap cannot be spanned by good works, charitable giving, religion or anything of human effort. That verse which says we have all sinned and fallen short of God's glory means we all miss the mark, failing to reach the standard.

Imagine it this way: All humanity stands on the shore of America's West Coast. Each person's goal is to jump in the water and swim to Hawaii. Some will only be able to wade out a short distance, others will brave the currents and progress beyond the breakers. A few will swim several miles. But no one will make it all the way to Hawaii, for none possesses the ability. So it is with our ability to reach God's standard. Since we cannot, death is the consequence . . . unless God provides another way.

God, who knows and loves each of us immeasurably in spite of our sinfulness, has provided a way, a way for fellowship with Him to be restored fully. It is a way for us to receive and enjoy His life—eternally. Yes, "the wages of sin is death," but the verse goes on to say: ". . . but the gift of God is eternal life."

How did God do this? Through the person of Jesus Christ He Himself became the way. As God, as our perfect substitute, Jesus took our place and bore our sin, thus fulfilling God's demand. Jesus Christ never sinned and therefore did not deserve condemnation—but He received it for our sake. He took our penalty upon Himself, giving His life willingly.

How is it possible to receive the life Jesus has made possible? Certainly not by good works. Ephesians 2:8–9 says, "For it is by grace you have been saved, through faith, and this is not from yourselves, it is the gift of God, not by works so that no one boast." So God is saying that if we could do anything to

174 * THE WAY OUT

save ourselves we'd brag about it! The only way is through faith—placing our trust in Jesus Christ alone. He Himself said, "I am the way, the truth and the life. No one comes to the Father except through me" (John 14:6).

The result of believing and receiving Jesus Christ as your personal Savior is not only the promise of life in heaven. It also means an abundant, purposeful life right here on earth. Through Him there is the joyful assurance of complete forgiveness and peace. The change He brings is a spiritual revolution, a new birth to a new life. It relates to every facet of life—even sex.

Teri is sixteen. She is experiencing the reality of new life in Christ: "Knowing Christ has made it very easy to make a decision about sex. Just knowing that Christ is watching has made not having sex now a natural choice. Since I received Christ I've lived a different life. I'm proud of it."

Knowing Jesus Christ early in life can be a tremendous advantage, guarding young people from the dangers of the teenage years. For those who have pursued their own desires and found them empty, there's a fresh new start when they meet Christ. One high school senior who has turned from a past of sexual experimentation told me: "God has totally changed my life. Since I've asked Him to save me and forgive me I've realized what I was doing and I stopped."

The fullness and purpose of life found through commitment to Jesus Christ is unparalleled. Far beyond rules and religion, true Christianity is a relationship to a Person, who gives His life to anyone who believes in and receives Him. One teenager told me: "Knowing Jesus Christ has made me assured that someone up there appreciates my decision to live differently from the mold. Knowing it is His will for me makes it a joy to live that way."

Another said: "Having sex before marriage was always wrong. Receiving the Lord into my life has really had an impact on my life. His love is enough to say no."

Going all the way in this sex-crazy world of ours means going all the way to destruction, dissatisfaction, and ultimate death. Choose the other path. Go all the way with Jesus Christ.

He is the key to your love life and the only Way to live happily ever after. If you want your sins forgiven, if you want peace and purpose in your life, if you want to go to heaven when you die, pray this simple prayer:

> Dear God,
>
> I know that I'm a sinner. I believe Jesus Christ died and rose from the dead for me. Right now, by faith, I invite Him to come into my life and save me. Thank You for the gift of eternal life. Thank You for the assurance that I am part of Your family and will go to heaven when I die. In Jesus' Name, Amen.

If you would like more information about experiencing this new beginning in your life, or if you have a question about anything presented in this book, feel free to contact me. My address is P. O. Box 12193, Overland Park, KS 66212. Telephone (913) 492–2066.

A personal word from Jerry Johnston . . .

SEX IS ALWAYS MORE THAN SEX!

It is more than just an exhilarating "physical" kick. And its misuse can bring some pretty heavy effects on what was once a happy and carefree life:

* EMOTIONAL HANGUPS
* GUILTY CONSCIENCE
* PREGNANCY
* HATE AND ANGER
* ABORTION
* FEAR OF DISEASE
* THOUGHTS OF SUICIDE

Yes, teenager, "sex is always more than sex" and in perspective . . . it is supposed to be.

But there are times when life can just plain hurt. The knot in your stomach is real. Why? And . . . why me? you ask.

It is really important that you know that you are *not* alone. There are others who have been right where you are . . . right now!

Standing by right now are special friends of mine who are professionally trained to help you deal with the guilt, the emotions, the pain.

They are friends who really care. Friends who want to help you . . . right now! Pick up the telephone and call my hotline now. It is a free call regardless of how long you need to talk.

1 800 SV.–A–TEEN

(1–800–782–8336)

We care about you and your future!

NOTES

* * *

Introduction

1. Patricia Hersch, "Coming of Age on City Streets," *Psychology Today,* (January, 1988), 34.
2. Bettie B. Youngs, Ph.D., *Helping Your Teenager Deal With Stress* (New York: St. Martin's Press, 1986), 126.
3. Ibid., 135.
4. Dr. Ruth Westheimer and Dr. Nathan Kravetz, *First Love* (New York: Warner Books, 1985), 205.
5. David Elkind, *All Grown Up & No Place to Go* (Reading: Addison-Wesley Publishing Company, 1984), 62.

Chapter 1

1. *Redbook,* September, 1987, Special Survey Results, 148.
2. Ibid.
3. Ibid.
4. Ibid.
5. *Sexually Transmitted Diseases,* 1985, Worldwide Church of God, 1.
6. Ibid., 1.
7. Leslie Roberts, Science, "Sex and Cancer," July /August 1986, 30.
8. *Sexually Transmitted Diseases,* 11.
9. Ibid., 4.
10. Ibid., 4.
11. Ibid., 3.
12. Ibid., 5.
13. Ibid., 11.
14. Ibid., 6.
15. "The New Scarlet Letter," *Time,* 2 August 1982, 62.
16. *Sexually Transmitted Diseases,* 3.
17. Roberts, 30.
18. *The Seattle Times,* Warren King, *Times* medical reporter, Sunday, 7 June 1987, B2.

Chapter 2

1. David Van Biema, "What's Gone Wrong with Teen Sex," *People Magazine* (13 April 1987), 111.
2. Special Report, Alan Guttmacher Institute, 1985.
3. "School Contraceptives," *Kansas City Star* (10 October 1986), 2A.
4. Van Biema, 112.
5. Van Biema, 115.
6. Van Biema, 115.
7. Van Biema, 119.
8. Cheryl McCall, "Denises's Decision" *Life* (March, 1986), 72.
9. Vanessa J. Gallman, "Mother to Mother" *Essence* (May, 1986), 134.
10. Search Institute Source, Vol. 1, Nov., 1985, 1.
11. Ibid.
12. Ibid.
13. Gallman, 134.
14. "Babies Having Babies," *Life* (December, 1983) 108.
15. Ibid., 112.
16. Ibid., 108.
17. Ibid.
18. Source, 1.
19. "It's Saturday Night" *Life* (March, 1986), 33.

Chapter 3

1. Roberts Pugh, Landrum B. Skittles, *From Conception to Birth* (New York: Harper & Row Publishers, 1973), 53.
2. David Jeremiah, *Before It's Too Late* (Nashville: Thomas Nelson, 1982), 46.
3. Jeremiah, 43.
4. Ibid., 30.
5. Cornerstone (Volume 8, Issue 49, n.d.), 31.
6. Curt Young, *The Least of These* (Chicago: Moody Press, 1983), 29.
7. Don Baker, *Beyond Choice* (Portland, OR: Multnomah Press, 1985), 29–31.

Chapter 4

1. *World Almanac* (New York: World Almanac Press, 1987), 368–369.
2. Donald Wildmon, *The Case against Pornography* (Wheaton, IL: Victor Books, 1986), 35.
3. Ibid., 24.
4. "Porno Plague Hits Cities," *U.S. News and World Report,* 4 September 1985, 46.
5. Ibid., 46.

Chapter 5

1. Search Institute Source (January, 1986), 1.
2. Ibid.
3. George M. Beschner and Alfred S. Friedman, *Youth Drug Abuse* (Lexington, Mass.: D.C. Health and Company, 1979), 78–100.
4. Lynn Darling, "Everybody's Gone Dating" *Mademoiselle* (February, 1986), 122.
5. "Making Sense of Your Sexual History," *Cosmopolitan* (August, 1986), 181.
6. *Jet* (25 June 1984), 52.
7. Shere Hite, *The Hite Report on Male Sexuality* (New York: Alfred A. Knopf, 1981), 721.
8. Ibid., 722.
9. Beschner and Friedman, 203–207.
10. Personal Interview.
11. Personal Interview.
12. Personal Interview.
13. Personal Interview.
14. Ibid., Source.
15. Personal Interview.

Chapter 6

1. "Then I had this day . . ." *Discover* (July, 1987), 18.
2. Shere Hite, *The Hite Report on Male Sexuality* (New York: Alfred A. Knopf, 1981), 712.
3. Ibid., 717.
4. Ibid., 718.
5. Ibid., 721.
6. Ibid., 728.
7. Ibid., 729.
8. "Study Shows . . ." *The Kansas City Star* (22 September 1985), 1A.
9. Ibid.
10. "Date Rape . . ." *Psychology Today* (July, 1987), 10.
11. "Victim tells . . ." *The Kansas City Times* (9 October 1987), B1.

Chapter 7

1. "Sex in the Ivy League" *Newsweek* (24 March 1986), 61.
2. Shere Hite, *The Hite Report on Male Sexuality* (New York: Alfred A. Knopf, 1981), 767.
3. Ibid., 768.
4. Ibid.
5. *Attorney General's Commission on Pornography* (Nashville: Rutledge Hill Press, 1986), 297.

6. "Heterosexuals and AIDS" *Atlanta Monthly* (February, 1987), 46.
7. Ibid.
8. Ibid.
9. Ibid., 47.
10. Ibid.
11. Ibid.

Chapter 8

1. Louise Armstrong, *Kiss Daddy Goodnight* (New York: Simon and Schuster, 1987), 108.
2. Ibid., 84.
3. Ibid., 61.

Chapter 9

1. Edmund White, *States of Desire* (Toronto, Canada: Clarke, Irwin and Co., 1980), 8.
2. Ibid., 283.
3. Ibid., 279.
4. Ibid., 18.
5. Ibid., 40.
6. Ibid., 120.
7. Ibid., 145.
8. Ibid., 52.
9. Ibid., 135.
10. Ibid., 267.
11. John Rechy, *City of Night* (New York: Grove Press, 1963), 43.
12. James Dobson, *Love Must Be Tough* (Waco, Texas: Word, Inc., 1983), 164–165.
13. Rechy, 97.
14. White, 36.

Chapter 10

1. Patricia Bosworth, "Let's Call It Suicide," *Vanity Fair* (March, 1985), 52.
2. Bosworth, 53.
3. *Attorney General's Commission on Pornography* (Nashville: Rutledge Hill Press, 1986), 501.
4. Ibid., 500.
5. Ibid.

Chapter 11

* Gene Antonio, *The AIDS Cover-Up* (San Francisco: Ignatius Press, 1986).
1. "You Haven't Heard Anything Yet" *Time* (16 February 1987), 54.

2. "AIDS: A Look into the Future" *USA Today* (1 June 1987), 6D.
3. Steve Findlay, *USA Today* (3 June 1987), D1.
4. Ibid.
5. "AIDS: A Look into the Future," 6D.
6. "New AIDS Policy" *The Maui Press* (9 June 1987), A6.
7. "Positive AIDS Tests . . ." *The Honolulu Advertiser* (9 June 1987), A8.
8. "Hidden AIDS" *USA Today* (25 June 1986), 5D.
9. "AIDS Insurance" *Newsday* (10 July 1986), 79.
10. "AIDS alters sex habits . . ." *USA Today* (15 December 1986), 6D.
11. "AIDS fear hurts . . ." *The Dallas Morning News* (25 November 1985), 20A.
12. "AIDS fears . . ." *USA Today* (28 August 1985), 1A.
13. "Cops wearing rubber gloves . . ." *San Francisco Examiner* (_ June 1987), A1.
14. "AIDS: A Look into the Future," 6D.
15. "Face of AIDS" *Newsweek* (10 August 1987), 22.
16. Ibid.
17. Lisa Krieger, *San Francisco Examiner* (5 June 1987), A6.
18. "Face of AIDS" *Vancouver Sun* (6 June 1987), 1.
19. Ibid.
20. Ibid.
21. Ibid., A11.
22. Steven Findlay, *USA Today* (16 October 1985), 10.
23. Lisa Krieger, *San Francisco Examiner* (6 June 1987), A4.
24. *Atlanta Constitution* (26 October 1985), 16A.
25. *Newsweek* (10 August 1987), 25.
26. "Many aren't getting . . ." *USA Today* (8 June 1987), 6D.
27. *Newsweek* (7 September 1987), 52.
28. Ibid.
29. *Newsweek* (10 August 1987), 22.
30. *USA Today,* "A Look into the Future," June 1987, 60.

Chapter 12

1. Sally Helms and Robert Tenenbaum, "Kids and Sex" *Columbu. Monthly* (no date), 60.
2. Ibid.
3. Andy Secher, "Motley Crue: The Sleaze Patrol" *Hit Parader,* (June, 1984), 16.
4. Andy Secher, "Motley Crue: The Wild Bunch" *Hit Parader,* (August, 1984), 20.
5. "Anatomy of a Relationship" *Cosmopolitan* (August, 1986), 214.

Chapter 13

1. *Charlotte Observer* (5 November 1986), 1.
2. "Divorce Warriors" *The Kansas City Times* (June, 1987), 27.

3. *Atlanta Constitution* (28 August 1987), 9A.
4. "Teen Sex" *People Magazine* (13 April 1987), 111.

Chapter 14

1. Curt Young, *The Least of These* (Chicago: Moody Press, 1983), 12.
2. Ibid., 13.
3. David Jeremiah, *Before It's Too Late* (Nashville: Thomas Nelson, 1982), 51.
4. Ibid., 51–52.
5. Young, 15.
6. Jeremiah, 52.
7. Ibid., 49.
8. Young, 16.
9. Ibid., 27.

Chapter 15

1. Donald E. Wildmon, *The Home Invaders* (Wheaton, IL: Victor Books, 1985), 126.
2. Ibid., 132.
3. "Television Sex and Violence" *Parents* (July, 1986), 60.
4. "Chase Out of Town" *People Magazine* (11 May 1987), 105.
5. Ibid.
6. "Children Having Children" *Time* (9 December 1985), 81.
7. Ibid.
8. Sally Helms and Robert Tenenbaum, "Kids and Sex" *Columbus Monthly,* (April, 1980), 60.

Chapter 16

1. *Circus* (7 July 1977), 40.
2. Tipper Gore, *Raising PG Kids in an X-rated World* (Nashville: Abingdon Press, 1987), 84.
3. Dan and Steve Peters, *Why Knock Rock?* (Minneapolis: Bethany House Publishers, 1984), 185.
4. Peters, 185.
5. Ibid., 87.
6. Ibid., 86.
7. Ibid., 87.
8. Ibid., 89.

Chapter 17

1. "Poll Shows Support for Sex Education" *The Kansas City Star* (8 October 1981), 8A.
2. Sally Helms and Robert Tenenbaum, *Columbus Monthly,* "Kids

and Sex" (no date), 51.

3. Tim LaHaye, *Sex Education Is for the Family* (Grand Rapids: Zondervan, 1985), 18.
4. George F. Will, "Sex Educators on the Rampage" *Conservative Digest* (July, 1979), 10.
5. Roger Libby, "Teach About Sex in a Positive Way," *USA Today* (16 March 1987), 12A.
6. Planned Parenthood, *How to Talk with Your Child About Sexuality* (Garden City: Doubleday Co., Inc., 1986), 118–120.
7. John Quinn, Ed., "Teaching About Sex Protects Our Children" *USA Today* (16 March 1987), 12A.

Chapter 18

1. Sally Helms and Robert Tenenbaum, "Kids and Sex," *Columbus Monthly* (n.d.), 50.
2. Ibid.
3. Ibid., 50.
4. Dee Snider and Philip Bashe, *Dee Snider's Teenage Survival Guide* (Garden City: Doubleday, Inc., 1987), 63.
5. "Kids and Sex," 59.

Chapter 25

1. Anthony Carr, Liberty Report, (February, 1987), 3.
2. Ibid., 4.

Chapter 26

1. Research Ministries Report, Vol. I, Issue 1, 3.
2. 1 Corinthians, MacArthur New Testament Commentary, (Chicago: Moody Press, 1984), 339.
3. *Moody Monthly* (July/August, 1987).

SUBJECT INDEX

ABOUT THE AUTHOR

In over 1,000 cities across the United States and Canada, Jerry Johnston has spoken to 3,000,000 teenagers in 2500 public schools. Jerry is considered an authority on the teenage culture. He has addressed the vital issues confronting youth on countless national radio and television programs throughout North America. Johnston's organization based in Kansas City counsels with troubled youth weekly via their nationwide hotline, 1–800-SV.–A–TEEN (1–800–782–8336). This hotline is an extension of his speaking in high schools and entails counseling materials, guidance, and a full adolescent residential recovery program if needed.

President Reagan and educators from coast to coast have praised Johnston's message and work because of the profound impact it is making on young people everywhere.

Why Suicide?, a book on the teenage suicide epidemic, is another book authored by Jerry Johnston. Jerry, his wife, Christie, and their three children, Danielle, Jeremy, and Jenilee live in Kansas City.

For further information, please write: Jerry Johnston Association, P. O. Box 12193, Overland Park, KS 66212–0193.